*T*o all the humble beasts that be,

To all the birds on land and sea,

Great Spirit, sweet protection give,

That free and happy they may live.

John Galsworthy

Opossum

VIRGINIA OPOSSUM
(Didelphis virginiana)

The Virginia opossum is the only marsupial found in the United States. The babies of marsupials do not fully develop in their mother's womb like the young of other animals. Instead, they are expelled from the womb at a very early stage and continue their development in an external pouch. (Not all marsupials have pouches. The babies of some marsupial species just hang onto their mother's nipples without the protection of a pouch.)

Opossum is correctly pronounced with the "O," although the common slang is "possum." "Possum" is not technically correct because there are other mammals from Australian and Asia that are actually called possums.

With its pointed snout, two-foot body, and foot long, hairless tail, an opossum looks a bit strange. Captain John Smith of the Pilgrims wrote of them that they have "a head like a Swine and a taile like a Rat."

Opossums are shy, solitary animals. They come together only to mate, and the males leave immediately after mating.

Always common in the eastern United States, except the northernmost states, the opossum has spread as far north as Canada and as far west as New Mexico. It has been introduced to the Pacific Coast. The opossum is so adaptable and has adjusted so well to humans that it has thrived while many other mammals saw their numbers and range decline. Now it can even be found in large cities.

△ When the surviving babies are only slightly bigger than a mouse, they wander out of the pouch and hang onto the hair on their mother's back and neck. They do not hang onto their mother's tail, as cartoons and drawings often suggest. They go back to the pouch to nurse. After another month or so they can care for themselves, and they wander off. Possums are not territorial but roam from place to place seeking food. Carrying their babies on their backs enables the females to roam about without having to return home in order to care for their young.

THE MARSUPIAL POUCH

Virginia opossums have an external pouch in which they carry their incompletely developed young. In Florida, they usually have two litters yearly. The fertilized eggs develop into embryos in the uterus and are born 12 to 14 days after conception.

Upon birth, the baby opossums move out of the womb and crawl several inches

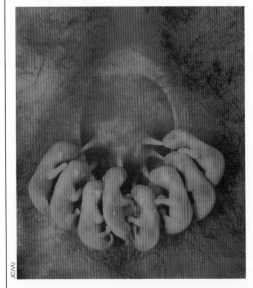

forward into their mother's fur-lined pouch. This is surely one of nature's marvels. The newborn opossums are blind, but their front legs are relatively well developed with claws which aid the trip to the pouch. They are extremely tiny, so small that 20 would fit on one teaspoon and 200 weigh only an ounce. Nevertheless, they make their way to the pouch (one trip was recorded at only 17 seconds), grab onto a teat, and hang on for 2 to 3 months. Sometimes more babies are born than the mother has teats (the number of teats can vary from the usual 13 up to 17), resulting in death for those unfortunate few for whom there is no nipple. Usually, in spite of the large number of teats, there are only 7 to 8 young in the pouch.

The young are normally found inside the pouch. The photographer in this case lifted the young outside and arranged them so it was possible to see them holding the nipples. The babies stay attached to their mother's nipples at all times until they leave the pouch. If they let go, they are doomed.

◁ The opossum's tail is prehensile (capable of grasping). The tail is used for balance, support, and to carry material for nest building, but usually only young opossums can actually support their weight and hang from their tail. The opossum is the only native mammal in the United States that has a grasping tail, although many mammals in other parts of the world, such as monkeys, have this kind of tail.

PEA BRAINS

This photo shows a human skull alongside the skull of an opossum. Opossums have the smallest brain/weight ratio of any mammal in North America. By comparison, a raccoon of the same body weight has a brain six times larger. Humans have the largest brain relative to their body size. Animals with larger brains, such as dolphins and primates, seem to be more intelligent. The definition of intelligence is very subjective, and intelligence is usually measured by the ability to learn from humans or to solve problems devised by humans. However, the ability to adapt to their environment is the means by which mammals survive in the wild. Because of its adaptability, the opossum has not only succeeded in expanding its range, but has also managed to survive in environments that have been greatly altered by humans.

THE IMMIGRANT

Long ago, North and South America were completely separate and had different animals. Later, they became connected by a land bridge (Panama), and animals moved from each continent to the other. Although the more successful migration was southward, a few South American mammals were able to compete and survive in North America. The opossum was one of the few that prospered. Other successful South Americans include the armadillo and porcupine.

▷ Opossum characteristics include a pink nose, naked black ears with white tips, and prominent whiskers.

△ Young opossums can be easily tamed but they don't make good pets. They are not affectionate animals and can be unpredictable and nasty as adults.

Opossum

Opossums eat many kinds of plants and animal matter, dead or alive, including garbage, so they generally have little trouble finding food. Their diet includes fruits, vegetables, nuts, seeds, eggs, worms, small fish, insects, mice, and frogs. They even eat rattlesnakes. (Opossums are immune to the poisonous venom of America's pit vipers.)

Although very few live to be two years of age, opossums may live seven years or more, and if not killed they continue to grow. Adults may weigh up to ten pounds in Florida, with an exceptional one reaching fifteen pounds. In captivity, one is reported to have reached a weight of more than thirty pounds.

Natural enemies include owls, bobcats, hawks, panthers, and especially dogs. However, these predators will only eat an opossum in extreme hunger. In fact, man is one of the few creatures that will eat an opossum when other food is available. "Possum and taters" was a popular food for early Florida settlers. Vultures don't mind eating possum roadkill.

Male opossums often fight ferociously. As a result, many are badly scarred, have scaly tails, and are missing teeth and toes. Yet opossums constantly groom themselves and are considered very clean.

Today, the automobile probably causes the most opossum mortality in Florida. Opossums are attracted to highways during their nightly foraging by the presence of other roadkills, but they are near-sighted and have trouble seeing the approaching cars. In addition, they tend to freeze when cars approach. This tactic serves them well in the wild because their stillness may reduce the chance of attack by a predator, but it leaves them far more vulnerable to cars.

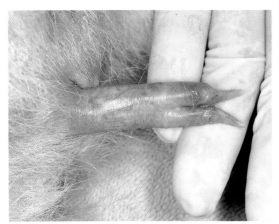

△ Female opossums have two uteruses; that's the meaning of the opossum's Latin name, *Didelphis*. Male opossums have a penis with a forked tip (shown above). Scientifically, the significance of this unusual anatomy is not clear. An interesting (but false) explanation from folklore is that opossums copulate through the female's nose.

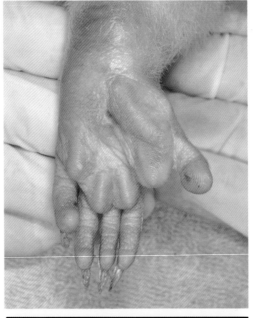

△ ▷ The shape of the opossum skull indicates the small size of this creature's brain. However, note the large number of teeth (50), more teeth than any other North American mammal except for some species of dolphins and porpoises. (Manatees have more than 50 teeth over the course of a lifetime but only 30 to 36 at any one time.)

△ This photo shows the trademark grimace of the opossum which is actually a threat display.

◁ △ The hind foot of the opossum has an opposable big toe which works like a human thumb for grasping. Note that it has no nail. With the aid of their tail, and their rear paws with opposable thumbs, opossums are good climbers. Opossum paw prints are distinctively star-shaped.

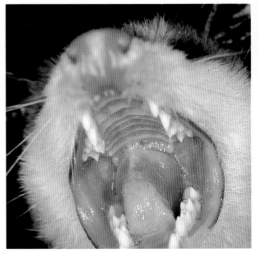

▽ The color of an opossum's fur varies from light to dark but is usually some combination of gray and brown.

4

Anatomically and physiologically, the opossum has attracted a lot of scientific attention. It is one of the most thoroughly studied animals of North America. The opossum evolved long after the dinosaurs, but its fossil record shows that it hasn't changed much for millions of years.

Opossums are popular research animals for drug studies relating to human gastrointestinal ailments, because they have a bile system which is very similar to that of humans. (Bile is produced by the liver and used in the small intestine.) In addition, they breed easily and produce many young, important features for research animals. Opossums are also useful in aging studies. They age very quickly, rarely living as long as two years.

PLAYING DEAD – AN OPOSSUM FOOLS THE AUTHOR

One day long ago, Barney, my pet fox terrier, found an opossum under the porch and dragged it out after a furious battle. The opossum, showing its full set of teeth, was bleeding from the mouth and coated with the dog's saliva. It was very still. Feeling certain the animal was dead, I ran to fetch my dad, to show him this strange creature I had never seen before. Barney had lost interest and followed me. When we returned, the opossum was gone without a trace. I earnestly declared that there really had been a dead animal right there. Gently, my dad explained that "possums" play dead. As Barney found out, a dead "possum" is no fun and not very appetizing, so the animal escaped with its life.

Feigning death is a defensive tactic used by some birds and reptiles but much less common among mammals. When opossums play dead, they go into a faint, properly called "catatonia," during which their heart rate and their breathing slows. They lie on their side, with their mouth open and their eyes closed. They don't respond even if they are poked sharply. This condition may last from less than a minute to several hours and seems to be a reflexive action over which the opossums have no control.

This defensive maneuver only works with predators who insist on live prey, but opossums have other defenses, too. They discourage attackers by snarling viciously and baring their teeth, and they can deliver a nasty bite. A strong odor from their anal glands also aids in their defence.

A DIFFERENT OPOSSUM

A short-tailed opossum (from South America) is shown here for contrast because, unlike the Virginia opossum of Florida, it has no functional pouch and must carry its young outside its body. These opossums are kept as pets in Latin America because they control household rodents.

Armadillo

NINE-BANDED ARMADILLO
(Dasypus novemcinctus)

The nine-banded armadillo, also known as the common long-nosed armadillo, ranges from the southern part of the United States through Central America into South America, as far south as Uruguay and Argentina. There are about 20 armadillo species in Central and South America. They range in size from the 7-inch fairy armadillo to the giant armadillo which can weigh 120 pounds. In the United States, there is only one species, the nine-banded armadillo. Armadillos are also known by such common names as "pocket dinosaurs," "Hoover hogs" (a reference to hungry people eating armadillos at the time of the Great Depression, during the presidency of Herbert Hoover), "Texas turkeys," and the rather insensitive names "road pizza" and "possums on the half-shell," both references to their tendency to be killed on highways.

The fossil record shows that various species of armadillos lived in Florida for several million years before becoming extinct about 10,000 years ago. The armadillos currently found in Florida have not been here very long, but they are now found throughout the state. Florida's armadillos have been traced to a natural, easterly movement of armadillos from Texas, starting about 1850, plus the offspring of several animals introduced on the

east coast of Florida between 1920 and 1936, including a pair which escaped from a small zoo in Cocoa, Florida. The offspring of the introduced animals have now populated the entire peninsula of Florida and have merged with armadillos expanding their range from the western states. The two populations probably met and merged somewhere in the panhandle during the 1970s.

△ The nine bands of the nine-banded armadillo are bands on the body, not the more obvious bands which appear on the tail. Other species of armadillos have different numbers of bands.

△ Orphaned baby armadillos are difficult to keep alive; they become anemic and bleed readily unless injected with vitamin K. In the daytime, a baby armadillo may faint or fall into a stupor for no apparent reason. Although its vital signs drop, it will recover in minutes or hours when aroused or hungry.

Armadillo means "little armored one," from the Spanish word *armado* meaning armored. The armor includes 9 bands of stiff, bony plates (hence the animal's name). These plates, which are covered by thin scales, protect the middle part of the animal. The tail is covered by scaly rings, and the head is protected by a shield. Armadillos also have hair, like all mammals. It is most plentiful on their undersides. Armadillos have tiny, peg-like teeth and long, hairless ears. They can live 10 to 15 years in the wild.

Armadillos are solitary animals that usually stay in underground burrows during the day and come out around dusk to forage for their favorite foods, beetles, and other invertebrates such as ants, millipedes, roaches and worms. They may also be predators of rare Florida reptiles such as the sand skink and worm lizard.

They have long, narrow, pig-like snouts and long tongues that flick out to lap up their prey. They have a ready supply of sticky saliva that helps in capturing insects. They dig very fast with muscular legs and long claws and can rapidly vanish into the ground. Darwin observed that an armadillo (although a different species) could disappear into the ground before a rider could dismount from his horse.

Each adult armadillo consumes an estimated 200 pounds of insects yearly. It can smell insects up to six inches underground. When it locates an insect, it tears up the soil with its strong legs and claws. This destructive digging behavior often upsets home owners and golf course greenskeepers, for obvious reasons. The armadillos' diverse diet includes amphibians, reptiles, and plant matter, in addition to insects. They sometimes eat the eggs of lizards and ground-nesting birds. In captivity, they are often fed raw, beaten eggs.

Armadillos can cross a body of water by walking along the bottom as they hold their breath or by swallowing air to inflate their intestines and then swimming across.

Some older Floridians can remember going "diller doggin" in their youth. This meant chasing armadillos along roadways, trying to catch them by their tails without

being clawed. It wasn't unusual for an unlucky armadillo to end up in a pot, its shell made into a beautiful, shellacked handbag to be sold to tourists. Armadillos are eaten in South America, where the gauchos call them traveling lunch boxes.

△ The soft underparts of the armadillo are not protected by the shell. Predators such as bobcats kill armadillos by rolling the animal onto its back and biting the unprotected stomach. To avoid this fate, armadillos roll into a ball (see page 8).

ARMADILLOS AS TROUBLEMAKERS

This a typical hole made by an armadillo. It detects its prey (usually beetles or their larvae) up to six inches underground with its keen sense of smell. It digs a hole with its forefeet and then sticks its long snout into the ground to capture the beetle with its sticky tongue. When a yard is destroyed by an armadillo, it may be best to smile and forgive these strange-looking, but fascinating, armored mammals for the temporary inconvenience they may cause, although it may be difficult to feel tolerant when an armadillo persists in tearing up a yard and plantings. The armadillo can be a real headache. But like many other animals, in pursuing its living in the way nature intended, it often comes inadvertently into conflict with humans. However, on the plus side, in addition to helping medical research, armadillos consume a lot of insects, aerate the soil, dig burrows that can be used by other animals, and as road kill, provide food for a number of scavengers.

Armadillos usually mate in the fall in Florida and give birth about four months later, but they may carry the very earliest stage of embryonic development, the blastocyst, for up to two years before it implants in the uterus and develops. They build a nest at the end of a short, underground tunnel in dry land, often in a cow pasture. They also use vegetation to build above-ground nests.

Armadillos almost always give birth to four identical young. They are the only mammal known to routinely have identical quadruplets, either four females or four males. The newborn have soft shells which harden progressively over a few weeks.

△ Armadillos are covered with a dome-shaped carapace consisting of bony plates which are covered with thin scales. This body covering is unique among living mammals.

△ The armadillo's armor may provide some protection against lesser predators such as small dogs, but larger predators such as panthers and alligators can bite through the shell. By rolling into a ball the armadillo can cover its stomach which has no armor, but its primary defence is to run into a burrow.

△ Note the open hole that these armadillos have dug. The armadillo detects insect prey with its keen sense of smell. It digs into the ground with its front paws and then sticks its snout into the hole to extract the insect, often a scarab beetle.

ARMADILLOS AS ROAD KILL

Although armadillos have a very acute sense of smell and hearing, their eyesight is quite poor. When disturbed by natural predators such as bears, coyotes, bobcats, panthers, dogs, and man, armadillos sit up and sniff the air in different directions, run wildly, or jump a couple of feet into the air, an instinctive reaction to avoid immediate attack. This tendency to jump when startled makes armadillos more vulnerable to cars. In many cases, an armadillo which would have been straddled harmlessly if it stood still was struck by an automobile's undercarriage when it leapt into the air. Road kills are probably the leading cause of armadillo mortality.

WHAT THE DOCTOR ORDERED

Armadillos are used for human leprosy research. Leprosy bacteria require body temperatures lower than those of common laboratory animals such as rats and mice. The armadillo's low body temperature makes it the ideal laboratory animal to test anti-leprosy drugs.

Armadillos from the southwestern United States may naturally carry the leprosy bacteria, but leprosy has never been reported in Florida armadillos. For this reason, researchers generally do not use wild armadillos from the west. They prefer Florida armadillos.

A laboratory in Melbourne, Florida, which is a center for leprosy research uses armadillos from the wild and also maintains a breeding colony. In any case, leprosy in armadillos is not a threat to humans, unless the infected animal is eaten.

△ Armadillos stand on their hind feet to better sniff the air for danger.

WHERE TO SEE ARMADILLOS

Wild armadillos can often be seen feeding along the sandy shoulders of highways in Florida. The Disneyworld exit from Interstate 4 is a reliable location to see armadillos as well as the eastern end of the Bee Line Expressway, and large parts of the Kennedy Space Center, especially the road leading to the Vehicle Assembly Building. The best time to look for them is late afternoon.

ARMADILLO FAN CLUB

The International Order of the Armadillo, P.O. Box 60305, Jacksonville, FL 32236, is a loose-knit organization of people fascinated with these strange creatures. It was founded by "dillo man" Bob Graessle. For a $10 membership fee, you get a decal, membership card, and a sheet with myths, legends, and facts about the armadillo.

Mole

EASTERN MOLE
(Scalopus aquaticus)

The eastern mole is abundant in every part of Florida where suitable soils occur except the Florida Keys. Due to its underground lifestyle, it is very difficult to study, so it is poorly understood in comparison to most other Florida mammals.

Moles mainly eat insects and earthworms and consume very little vegetation. Like shrews, moles must eat continuously day and night to maintain their high metabolic rate and constant physical activity.

Florida moles, like a number of other mammals, are much smaller than their counterparts in the Northeast or Midwest.

LIFE IN A TUNNEL

The known habits of the eastern mole revolve around its tunnel existence and its fossorial (underground) habits. A mole has huge, strong, front feet. The forelimbs are very short, which provides leverage for the powerful digging muscles. The special arrangement of bones and muscles causes the forepaws to be rotated, palms out. Its rear feet are small like those of a mouse. Using a twisting motion that may resemble swimming but which is an effective technique for excavation, the mole pushes dirt up and to the sides to form a tunnel. They often construct a myriad of tunnels just below the surface of the soil. These subsurface tunnels are used as a complex system of pitfalls for trapping insects, larvae and earthworms.

The mole also digs an interconnecting system of deeper tunnels, up to eighteen inches deep. Here it leads a mostly solitary life, interacting socially once a year to mate, build a nest, and raise a litter of young. The dirt from the deep tunnels is moved to the surface and expelled in such a way that a distinctive, volcano-shaped mound is formed with no plug over the opening.

Mole burrows are often distressing to farmers, golf course greenskeepers, and homeowners. Moles sometimes damage flower bulbs and crops. Even though moles do not usually eat vegetable matter, the digging activities of the mole cause roots to be loosened and exposed to air in the tunnels. This may cause plants to wither and die.

A mole does not patrol randomly but seems to be immediately aware of events throughout its vast tunnel network. When a hole is punched into a tunnel, for example, the mole immediately goes to make repairs. Also, when an insects drops through, the mole proceeds directly to the correct location to consume its prey.

A mole can bury itself in five seconds if placed on the ground. It can tunnel thirteen feet per hour near the surface. A single tunnel has been traced for 3,300 feet. The vast network of tunnels made by a single mole may cover one-half to two acres. The tunnels are repaired as needed and may be used for up to eight years before being abandoned, probably for lack of food. The mole's tunnel network is primarily a drop-trap for insects, the main food of the mole. Prey such as scarab beetles drop into the tunnels while digging in the soil. The mole's tunnels are thus different in purpose than those of the pocket gopher, which run slightly deeper and allow the gopher to eat roots.

It is fairly easy to distinguish the raised tunnels of moles from the diggings of other small, burrowing mammals. Mole tunnels are long ridges as shown in the photo. Mole hills or mounds are not common in Florida. Moles dig mounds in northern states where the soil is more moist. In Florida, moles are usually found in dry habitats.

Since a mole spends nearly its entire life in its tunnel system, its senses are developed very differently than those of mammals living above ground. The eyes of the eastern mole are completely covered by a membrane, allowing only light and dark to be sensed. A mole has no external ears, but its hearing is not impaired. The mole has a highly developed sense of touch which helps it adapt to life underground. The hairs on its snout, the top of its head, and the borders of its paws are highly sensitive and help the mole keep its bearings in the dark tunnels and also help it to detecting the presence of food items.

There is a lot that is still not known about eastern moles. It was formerly believed that moles were an agricultural nuisance because they damaged the roots of plants. Now it is thought that moles may actually benefit man by controlling insects and aerating the soil with their tunnels.

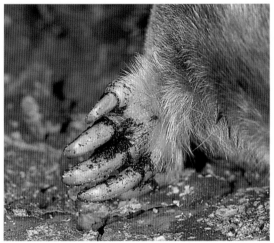

△ The powerful foot of the mole is used for digging and tunneling.

△ This photo shows a hairless baby mole. Baby animals that are born without hair are usually helpless for the first period of their lives and require a longer period of parental care. By comparison, baby jackrabbits are born fully furred and are able to run about soon after birth.

◁ The eastern mole has an eye which is not visible from the outside because it is covered with skin. However, it is believed that the mole can distinguish light from dark.

◁ This dissected view, with the skin stripped off, shows the mole's eye. Note the huge white nerve cord in front of the eye extending to the tactile hairs which are bunched in groups on the snout. For moles, the sense of touch is much more important that the ability to see.

MOLESKIN

The mole's coat of hair is unique in many ways. The mole's fur is among the most perfect of animal furs. The alternating round and flat segments of a single hair shaft make the coat extremely soft and capable of being bent forward and backward, thus reducing friction as the mole moves through its tunnels. Moleskin was very popular in Europe for making caps, purses, and tobacco pouches. In 1959, over one million moles were trapped for their skins in Britain alone. Since an eastern mole is only about six inches long (and European moles are similar in size), it took many skins to make anything of value. But the people who could afford these items appreciated the very fine fur. As late as the 1950s, moleskin was still popular with hikers to cover blisters. Synthetic materials have now replaced moleskin for this purpose.

CONFUSING COMMON NAMES

Many animals have different common names in different regions and languages. It is not unusual for a species to have dozens of common names worldwide. The species that Floridians commonly call panther, for example, is called by a variety of common names in other parts of the United States including mountain lion, cougar, puma and catamount. All these common names refer to just one animal whose scientific name is Felis concolor, meaning one-color cat.

Common names also introduce confusion when the name people in one region associate with a particular animal is applied to a completely different animal in another region. In Florida, the word "gopher" is usually used in reference to the gopher tortoise. The pocket gopher, which people in other regions would call gopher, is instead called a salamander here (which is probably derived from "sandy-mounder"), and the salamander called a spring lizard. Wood-peckers may be called wood chucks.

The confusion caused by common names is one of the reasons that scientists have chosen to assign each species a unique scientific (Latin) name which belongs to that species alone. This method of naming is very precise and allows scientists around the world to communicate accurately.

Animals that are biologically similar are grouped together. For example, all the animals in this book are mammals and belong to the Class Mammalia. Mammals share certain characteristics such as having hair or fur covering most of the body and having mammary glands which produce milk for the young.

The Class Mammalia is further subdivided into orders (for example, meat-eaters) and then families (one family of meat-eaters is cats). Finally, each animal is described by two Latin words indicating its genus and species.

Shrews

SHREWS

Three different shrews live in Florida. The southeastern shrew (*Sorex longirostris*) is rare, and while the least shrew (*Cryptotis parva*) and southern short-tailed shrew (*Blarina carolinensis*) are more common, they still are rarely seen. Sometimes a shrew may be uncovered in a decaying wood pile or found drowned in a swimming pool. Once in a while a cat is seen playing with a dead shrew. But, generally, shrews remain unseen in Florida. They are more common in northern Florida and far more common in cooler climates. They are found throughout the United States, Canada, and even Alaska.

Shrews have small eyes, and their vision is probably poor. They shut their eyes when eating. Their ears are also small or externally invisible, yet shrews can communicate vocally with other shrews. In addition, they emit a series of clicks and twitters which may serve as a system of echolocation. However, smell, taste, and tactile sensations are more important for shrews than sight and hearing.

Near the bottom of the mammalian food chain, shrews are eaten primarily by owls, and some are killed by dogs and cats, although some predators avoid them because of their scent glands. Shrews themselves eat all kinds of animal matter, including insects, earthworms, spiders, and small vertebrates such as frogs and mice. The young are born with their adult teeth, unlike most other mammals, so they are immediately able to chew and digest their prey without assistance from their parents.

△ Least shrew eating a cricket. Shrews eat large numbers of insects.

Each shrew may consume its own body weight every 24 hours. With a heart rate of about one thousand beats per minute, an extremely high rate of metabolism, and tiny size, shrews must eat every one to two hours to stay alive. Unless researchers check live traps hourly, they are likely to find only dehydrated, starved, dead shrews.

Shrews move very quickly to viciously attack and eat almost any small creature that doesn't kill them first, including mice much larger than themselves, and even other shrews. Given their prodigious appetites, shrews eat enormous numbers of harmful pests during their lifetime. It is said that 40 pounds of shrews eat the

△ Nest of shrews showing the small size of the hairless young.

FLORIDA'S FASCINATING ANIMALS

"*Florida has one of the most diverse and fascinating selection of fauna (animals) of any of the states,*" says Ron Nowak, a noted wildlife authority and the author of a very highly regarded book on the mammals of the earth. *Florida's most interesting creatures include a variety of rodents and bats, a large number of aquatic mammals, endangered and rare subspecies such as the Florida panther and the Key Largo woodrat, and species which fairly recently moved into Florida on their own, such as the armadillo and the coyote. Florida also has extirpated species that have been reintroduced, such as the bison, and a number* of introduced exotic species, possibly as many as 15. No other state has primates (monkeys), but two species have been introduced to Florida. *Although the introduction of exotics increases the diversity of animals in the state, these non-native species can have a negative effect on the environment and on the native species (see box on introduced species, page 118). The Florida peninsula is surrounded by water and enjoys a subtropical climate, while the panhandle has the climate and vegetation of an eastern forest. This diversity supports a broad range of mammals, from the diminutive key deer to the black bear.*

same amount of food as 90 pounds of mice or a 1,000 pound moose. However, these small animals are so seldom seen that most people are completely unaware of their existence, and even researchers have trouble finding them.

Least shrews weigh as little as a dime and have bodies measuring about two inches in length, plus a short stubby tail. Unlike other shrew species, least shrews often nest together. Occasionally they make a colonial nest in bee hives, giving them the nickname "bee shrew." They get along well enough that they can live together in colonies without killing one another, unlike the other species which will kill each other when housed together. They are the one of the most intensively studied of the shrews species.

△ Earthworms make up a large part of the diet of least shrews.

Short-tailed shrews, also well-studied in captivity and in the field, measure about four inches in length. The short-tailed shrew has a large gland on its belly which is used for communication during courtship and copulation. Like most shrew species, it also has glands on its sides that emit substances presumably used for marking territory and discouraging predators.

As if their voracious appetites and their killing techniques were not enough to earn the diminutive shrews a wicked reputation, the short-tailed shrew also has a paralyzing chemical in its saliva which is introduced into the bite wounds of its prey. This chemical causes lowering of the blood pressure, slowing of the heart beat, and trouble with respiration, thus weakening the victim and making it easier to kill. While not dangerous to man, the saliva from a shrew bite can cause great pain. As with many shrew species, short-tailed shrews may eat their kills immediately or cache them in burrows for future use. Not a bad idea if you must eat around the clock to stay alive.

In natural surroundings, shrews live only about 18 months, testimony to the rapid pace of their lives.

△ The southeastern shrew shown above can be distinguished from the other Florida shrew species by its long, bare snout, and longer tail. It is the smallest of the Florida shrews and one of Florida's rarest mammals.

TAMING OF THE SHREW

The word shrew in modern English means a scolding or vexatious woman. Even the word shrewd, which now means having sound judgment, in earlier times was used to describe a person who was sly, cunning, and generally villainous.

How did a small, mouse-like, insect-eater inspire such strong language? In old English folklore, shrews were blamed for various maladies of horses and cattle, particularly any paralysis or numbness of the legs. The following quote from a book published in the 1600s shows the unpleasant reputation the animal unfairly suffered at that time: "It beareth a cruel mind, desiring to hurt anything, neither is there a creature it loveth… they take their prey by deceit…They love the rotten flesh of a raven. If any horse…feeds in a pasture or grass in which a shrew has put forth her poison, it will presently die."

The short-tailed shrew is actually a ferocious mammals and its bite is painful. Both male and female shrews are aggressive. The word shrew was originally applied equally to both sexes of humans and also meant to berate or curse (to beshrew someone). Later, shrew came to mean only a scolding woman. Shrews in the wild produce high-pitched squeaks. Perhaps this harsh noise which could be compared to the sounds of a quarrelsome female might have inspired the modern meaning. Shakespeare enshrined forever this use of the word in one of his most popular plays without ever actually mentioning the animal.

Bats

Bats are the only mammals that can fly. Flying squirrels glide but do not really fly.

Bats belong to the order of mammals called Chiroptera, which, translated from Latin, means "hand-wing." Arm-and-leg-wing would be a more appropriate name because the membrane that creates the bat's wing extends from the arm to the leg and even to the tail.

Florida's bats are small, with a 6-10 inch wingspan, and weigh about an ounce. Small size is an advantage for bats, because for an animal to be able to fly, its wing surface must be proportional in size to its weight.

All the bats of Florida are insect-eaters. In other parts of the world, there are also fish-eating bats, fruit-eating bats, and vampire bats which drink blood from cattle and other animals.

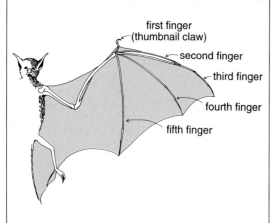

△ Part of the secret of bats' ability to fly is the modification of their hands through the lengthening of the finger bones.

first finger (thumbnail claw)
second finger
third finger
fourth finger
fifth finger

△ This big brown bat has a complete tail membrane. Unlike the free-tailed bats, its tail does not extend beyond the stretched membrane. Note that this bat has just caught a flying beetle.

△ When a bat is at rest, its mouth is closed, but during flight, it must open its mouth to use its echolocation and to catch food. This head shot of a big brown bat shows its fierce-looking teeth. Bats use these teeth to capture, hold, and chew insects. Large and sharp teeth are necessary because some insect prey have hard-shelled bodies (exoskeletons). Bats bite humans only in self-defence when cornered or picked up. Contrary to common belief, bats are no more likely to carry rabies than the other potential wildlife carriers such as raccoons, skunks, and foxes.

UNNECESSARY FEARS ABOUT BATS

Generally, bats are harmless to humans, and most of what is feared about bats is based on myth. Bats may come close to people while chasing insects, but their echolocation allows them to fly with great precision. They don't attack people, get tangled in their hair, or land on people's heads. Nor do bats ordinarily bite people. Most bites, and they are few, result from the careless handling of sick or injured bats.

However, there is a possibility of rabies resulting from a bat bite. Many mammals are susceptible to the rabies virus and bats are among them, but the chance of getting rabies from a bat is extremely remote. Bats with rabies usually die quickly and rarely transmit the disease. Since 1946 only about 20 people in the United States have died from bat-transmitted rabies. Most of these were bitten while handling a sick bat. Falling coconuts have reportedly killed more people than that.

MEXICAN FREE-TAILED BAT
(Tadarida brasiliensis)

There are two species of free-tailed bats in Florida, Mexican and Wagner's mastiff. Free-tailed means that the tail sticks out beyond the membrane stretched between the hind legs. Thus, the tails of these bats more closely resemble the tails of other mammals. The other 14 species of Florida bats have membranes which extend to the tips of their tails. Free-tailed bats are among the fastest flyers of the bats. They have long, narrow wings and fly quite high.

The Mexican free-tailed bat is also commonly known as the Brazilian free-tailed bat. It is famous for living in huge colonies in natural caverns and also in man-made structures such as bridges. In the desert Southwest, tourists gather to watch dense clouds of these bats emerging from their roosts for their evening forays. Although the colonies in the Southwest are much larger than those in Florida (up to several million), one colony in Gainesville was found to contain over 10,000 bats.

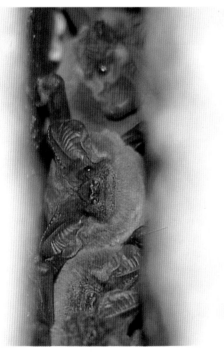

△ This photo shows Mexican free-tails roosting in the crevice between sections of a highway overpass, a common roosting site for this species in Florida.

△ This baby, orphaned Mexican free-tailed bat would ordinarily be found clinging to its mother but is now holding on to a twig instead.

△ This Mexican free-tailed bat's tail sticks out beyond the tail membrane. This feature is helpful for identification. Compare the tail of this bat with the tail of the big brown bat in flight in the photo at the top of page 14. The big brown bat in that photo is not a free-tailed bat and its membrane extends almost to the tip of its tail.

BAT HOUSES

To help protect these important and unique creatures, "bat houses," which are externally similar to bird houses, are now available from conservation organizations. Bats seem to prefer rough wooden surfaces to which they can cling easily. A 3/4 inch entry space is large enough to admit bats but small enough to exclude many predators. The idea of bat houses probably came from the observation that some bats occasionally roost in tree holes, and as old trees were knocked down, an alternative was needed.

FLYING MICE

Bats are sometimes called "flying mice," but this name is very misleading. The German word for bat is fledermause which means "flying mouse" and is enshrined in the title of Mozart's opera, Die Fledermause. The French word for bat is chauves-souris, meaning "bald mouse." Although they have soft fur, bats are not closely related to mice. Bats are also much less prolific than most mice, usually giving birth only once a year to a single offspring or twins. "Flying shrew" would be a comparison closer to reality.

MORE BAT SPECIES THAN...

Bats comprise more than 20% of all the mammal species on earth. About 900 of the over 4,400 species of mammals worldwide are bats. In some tropical countries, the number of species of bats is greater than all the other species of mammals combined. In spite of their impressive presence on this planet, we know very little about them. Man has devoted much more energy attempting to eradicate them than trying to understand them.

Bats

On a worldwide scale, bats are an important source of guano, or manure, which is used as fertilizer. They are also extremely important as pollinators of plants and dispersers of seed, something which was not understood or appreciated until fairly recently. However, no Florida bat is a nectar eater, so bats do not pollinate flowers in this state. But they are important in Florida as insect-eaters.

Approximately 70 percent of the world's bat species are insectivorous, feeding on moths, mosquitoes, flies, beetles, and other flying insects. Insectivorous bats often live near rivers, lakes, marshes, and swamps, because that's where insects are usually most numerous. All of the bats which breed in Florida feed on insects. There are persistent reports that Jamaican fruit-eating bats appear in the Keys at times, but they probably do not breed there.

DO BATS HELP CONTROL MOSQUITOS?

As the major predators of nocturnal flying insects in Florida, bats are ecologically among the most valuable mammals in Florida. Some people have asserted that bats are helpful in controlling mosquitos. It is true that some Florida bats feed on mosquitos at some times of the year, but no bats are known to eat mosquitos all the time. In fact, the details of bat feeding habits are not well known, so their usefulness in controlling mosquitos is still open to debate. Most likely, the rise and fall of mosquito populations are more dependant on other factors.

RED BAT
(*Lasiurus borealis*)

As its name implies, the red bat's fur is red in color, ranging from brick red to rusty red and sometimes even orange. Red bats are considered by some to be among the most beautiful mammals. Male red bats are more brightly colored than females but are slightly smaller. In Florida, red bats are found in the northern half of the peninsula but are less common than yellow and Seminole bats.

Red bats roost in the foliage of trees, usually hanging from a leaf, twig, or branch. This species is solitary for most of the year, except for the breeding season. Red bats are one of the bats most commonly seen feeding on insects around street lights. During cold periods in the winter, the red bat may wrap its furred tail membrane around the rest of its body to conserve heat and go into an inactive state called torpor.

△ This is a male red bat. Note that its color is brighter than that of the female at left. The female has a ring of light fur, starting at the neck, and has a duller, more grayish color.

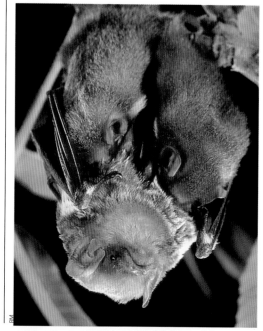

◁ This female red bat has two babies clinging to her. Notice that the babies are half the size of their mother but still suckling. The red bat is solitary for most of the year, except when the female has young. Florida bats (and most others) reproduce slowly compared to other mammals, usually producing only one or two young per year. Most other small mammals produce large litters, and their young are weaned quickly. However, baby bats grow slowly and need lots of maternal care and protection.

THE BAT MAN

*Bats are probably the most maligned group of mammals on the face of the earth. Although they have been widely persecuted, they were not seriously studied until the last several decades. Fortunately, as a result of the work of America's most famous "bat man," Dr. Merlin Tuttle, and other scientists and educators, many of the misconceptions surrounding bats are being corrected. Dr. Tuttle is the author of **America's Neighborhood Bats** and founder of the organization Bat Conservation International (BCI).*

BCI is the best source of information about bats. This exceptional organization, headed by Dr. Tuttle, has sponsored much of the recent work on bats. Anybody with questions about bats is welcome to write or call (P.O. Box 162603, Austin, Texas 78716, phone 512-327-9721, fax 512-327-9724). People wanting to become members may call toll-free, 1-800-538-BATS. BCI publishes a newsletter each month to let members know what the organization is doing.

NORTHERN YELLOW BAT
(Lasiurus intermedius)

The northern yellow bat is one of Florida's larger bats, although it is only 4 or 5 inches in length and weighs less than an ounce. Females are generally larger than males. The yellow bat has long wings and fairly short ears. As its name suggests, this bat has yellow fur, both above and below. Color variations range from yellowish-orange to yellowish-brown to almost gray. The long, silky fur covers about half of the tail membrane. Yellow bats are found primarily on the Atlantic and Gulf coastal plains of the southeastern United States, from Virginia to Texas, including Florida.

△ A bird's wing is formed by feathers, but a bat's wing is just bare membrane and the blood vessels can be seen. Bats flutter, but they cannot glide, because their wings are not broad enough.

Yellow bats are solitary for most of the year. Their preferred daytime roost is in clumps of Spanish moss hanging from trees, most commonly in long leaf pine and oak forests near a stream or lake. This bat rarely enters buildings or caves but is usually found where there is Spanish moss, in which it lives and gives birth to its young. Yellow bats, as well as seminole bats, were commonly encountered by professional moss gatherers, people who collected Spanish moss earlier in this century for stuffing mattresses and upholstery. In one study, a moss gatherer was reported to have found 50 yellow bats in a grove of live oaks less than an acre in size, including mothers carrying young.

Yellow bats tend to leave their roosts earlier than other Florida bats, often before dark. They feed on flying insects such as mosquitos, flies, and moths. Yellow bats mate in the fall, but fertilization is delayed throughout the winter months and does not take place until the following spring. Females generally leave their young in a clump of Spanish moss when they go out in the evening to feed, but when disturbed during the day, the mothers will carry their young with them.

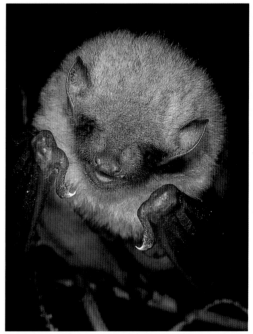

△ Bats have one claw on each wing which is a bat's version of the human thumbnail. The wing membrane is actually stretched between the bat's fingers. Bats hang upside down by their hind feet, which have sharp claws like those of a cat. The claw on each wing is not used for hanging but for grasping, to help the bat move around in its roost.

BAT CAVES

Several bat species in Florida roost in caves. The caves in which breeding females give birth and rear their young are called maternity caves. During the breeding season, the males and non-breeding females usually roost in separate caves called bachelor caves. These bats rejoin the colony after the young begin to fly.

Only certain caves are suitable for bats, because bats require fairly specific temperatures and humidities. The largest known maternity cave in Florida, in Jackson County in the Panhandle, is home to 100,000 adult females during the breeding season.

It is important to avoid disturbing maternity caves when bats are present. Most bats are timid creatures and are not able to tolerate much human intrusion. When people enter maternity caves during the breeding season, the bats often panic. Baby bats are knocked to the ground, where they fall prey to rats, mites, and cockroaches. Many bats prefer to roost over water, and their babies may drown. The females may even abandon the cave, leaving their young to die.

Many bat caves in Florida have been completely abandoned in the last 20 to 30 years. Of the 10 caves in Central Florida known to have housed bats for any length of time, only a few are still occupied. Some caves have been vandalized, destroyed by bulldozers, or sealed by property owners.

Grates have been used to keep people out of caves, but this has often been harmful to the bats. In some cases the grates reduced air circulation, and the caves became too warm for the bats to tolerate. In other cases, the bats were slowed down by the grates, making them more vulnerable to the many predators, such as owls, that often hang around cave entrances in search of an easy meal. Nevertheless, grates or fences are currently the only way to protect bats from people.

Natural disasters, especially floods, have also killed large numbers of bats. Flooding can fill a cave so quickly that an entire colony of bats is wiped out.

Bats roost on the ceiling of the cave, close together to conserve heat. There may be as many as 150 bats per square foot on the ceiling.

△ These photos show the ceiling of a bat cave in Texas covered with Mexican free-tailed bats. The same densities of Mexican free-tails (although not the same large numbers) can be observed in Florida where they roost in buildings and under bridges. This species does not roost in Florida caves, perhaps because the caves are too small or too humid. The species most often found in Florida caves are brown bats, gray bats, southeastern bats, and pipistrelles.

The mothers leave their young, huddled together, every night to hunt for food. When they return, hours later, they unfailingly locate their own babies among the thousands massed together on the ceiling. They apparently have excellent spatial orientation and can recognize their offspring's individual distress call, an amazing feat when it is considered that the largest colonies in other states contain as many as one million bats. Once reunited, the babies grab hold of their mothers and begin to nurse.

Cave explorers have contributed to the disturbance of bats in the past. Today, however, most cavers understand and help protect bats, especially those who are members of the National Speleological Society. The protection of maternity caves during the breeding season is especially important.

GRAY BAT
(Myotis grisescens)

Once found in a few caves in the Florida Panhandle and throughout the southeastern United States, gray bats are now endangered because so many of their caves have been sealed, destroyed, or disturbed. In Florida, one important cave has a population estimated to include 10,000 gray bats (plus 50,000 southeastern bats). Of all the gray bats in the United States, 95% roost in only nine caves.

Human intrusion is the main reason for the decline of these bats. Gray bats are very timid, and people entering a maternity cave during their breeding season often cause panic and may cause the cave to be abandoned.

Like so many endangered species, gray bats cannot recover easily when their numbers decline, because females only bear one offspring per year (starting in their second year). Many of the young also fall prey to rats, snakes, owls, opossums, raccoons, and other predators, often near the cave entrances when they are first learning to fly and are still some-what clumsy. Some gray bats may live to be 30 years old, however.

Each adult gray bat eats as many as 1,000 insects a night. Thus, bats from the one fairly small colony in the Panhandle may consume 10,000,000 insects in a single night. That's a lot of insects.

Gray bats migrate in August from warm summer caves in Florida to colder caves in Tennessee and Alabama where they hibernate for the winter.

EASTERN PIPISTRELLE
(Pipistrellus subflavus)

The eastern pipistrelle is Florida's smallest bat. Adults weigh only about ⅕ of an ounce. Pipistrelles are normally yellowish to yellowish-brown or golden in color, but the race in the Florida peninsula and southern Georgia is grayish to dark brown. Each of the individual hairs is tricolored: dark at the base, light in the middle, and dark again at the tip.

The eastern pipistrelle is widespread in eastern North America but is absent from the southern third of the Florida peninsula and from the Keys.

Like yellow and Seminole bats, the eastern pipistrelle is generally solitary and often roosts in Spanish moss in Florida. It also roosts among leaves. However, unlike those other two species, the pipistrelle is commonly found in caves in the northern half of Florida, especially in the winter months. It is seldom found in buildings.

This bat leaves its roost early in the evening. It has a characteristically erratic, fluttering flight.

VAMPIRE BATS

There are 3 species of bats in Central and South America that feed on the blood of other warm-blooded animals such as cattle. These bats are called vampire bats. There are no vampire bats in Florida. However, they did live in Florida thousands of years ago, based on fossils found in the northern part of the state.

△ Pipistrelles regularly hibernate during winter, although the temperature in Florida caves (about 65°F or 18°C) is too warm for most other species of bats to successfully hibernate. During hibernation, tiny droplets of water often collect on the fur of the pipistrelles which give them a white or silvery appearance. This water collects on bats of other species also, but since most of the other bat species are not true hibernators in Florida and move around their caves, they tend to shake off any water droplets. But the pipistrelle, which remains motionless in hibernation, collects a large amount of moisture as shown in this typical photo.

BAT TOWERS IN FLORIDA (IF YOU BUILD IT, WILL THEY COME?)

In the 1920s, a 30-foot tower was built by a land developer on Lower Sugarloaf Key. The tower was designed so bats could fly in and out easily, and its purpose was to attract bats to control the numerous mosquitos. The

idea was ingenious, and the tower was a landmark for a while. However, no bats were ever willing to settle in the tower. For one thing, bats are scarce in the Keys, due in part to a lack of fresh water. Another mosquito-control bat tower constructed along the Hillsborough River near Tampa was a landmark for many years until it recently burned.

The effectiveness of using bats to control mosquitos is debatable. Factors such as breeding conditions and wind direction are considered more important in determining the size of mosquito populations than predation. Purple martins were once credited with helping to control mosquitos, and many people built multi-story martin houses to attract them. Their effectiveness has since been discredited, and the promotion was shown to be a scheme to sell expensive birdhouses. However, bats are different because they hunt insects at night, so the research applied to the purple martins is not completely relevant. Conservationists have sometimes used the idea of mosquito control as a gimmick to help convince the public that bats are not evil creatures. This might be considered a bit of over-

statement in the promotion of a good cause.

Several years ago the University of Florida became aware that their fairly new stadium complex had become inhabited by Mexican free-tailed bats numbering in the thousands. After consultation with resident bat biologists and considerable study, an enlightened plan was devised. The University's athletic association funded the construction of a large bat house on the edge of the campus near Lake Alice. A professional bat-relocator was hired to exclude the bats from the sports stadiums by placing wire mesh over their entrances. At the same time, many of the bats were captured and placed in the bat house. Unfortunately, the bats did not remain in their new house. Instead, they took up residence in many older buildings on campus which also had resident bat colonies. However, the story is not yet finished. Several years later, a small colony of bats began living in the UF bat house after the building had been modified to restrict light penetration. They stayed only a short time, but biologists hope some will return.

Bats

All bats have eyes and can see well. But since they fly and feed at night, they use a highly refined system called echolocation to track flying prey and avoid obstacles in the dark. Bats emit high-pitched sounds as they fly. Using the reflected sounds, or echoes, bats can determine the location, distance, size, shape, and texture of an object, and even its speed if the object is moving. Scientists say that the bat's echolocation system greatly surpasses current human understanding and is far more sophisticated than any radar system man has built.

Bats rest during the day, individually or communally, in trees, caves, under bridges, and sometimes in attics and other man-made structures. When resting, they hang upside down by their rear feet. Bats have very specific light and temperature requirements for roosting. Often the only clue to the location of their roost is their feces or odor at an opening of their roost. Some bats are very vulnerable to human disturbance, yet they often use man-made structures for roosting. They also use areas around street lights as feeding areas because many insects are attracted to lights, and therefore there is an abundant food supply for bats.

Bats reproduce slowly. They bear live young and nurse them as do all mammals. Most females bear one offspring yearly, but some species normally have twins, and others quadruplets. Bats in northern climates may live 20 to 30 years in the wild, an unusually long life for such a small animal.

Bats are identified by hair color, ear shape, skull shape, number of teeth, wing pattern, and the shape of their nose. Some species in Florida are quite rare, and others appear to be rare because they are difficult to find.

BAT DETECTORS

Bats frequently emit chirps and squeaks that are much lower in frequency than those used for echolocation. Some of these sounds are audible to humans. Usually, these low-frequency sounds are alarm calls or sounds used for communication between bats. The echolocation sounds are usually higher in frequency and cannot be heard by most humans.

Scientists studying bats use bat-detectors, receivers capable of detecting high-frequency sounds and changing them into sounds within the normal range of human hearing. Since different kinds of bats echolocate at different frequencies, experts can identify bat species by their sound patterns.

DEALING WITH BAT PROBLEMS

It is not necessary to kill bats. There are ways of handling bat problems that are both humane and effective. Bats are protected under Florida law. Pest control companies are not allowed to exterminate bats but can discourage them from coming inside buildings.

Bats sometimes come inside homes through open windows or doors while chasing insects. Usually they cannot find anything to hang from, so they wind up on the floor. When a bat is seen floundering around on the floor, it doesn't necessarily mean that it is hurt or exhausted. Some bats cannot take off from the ground, but must climb up on something such as a tree and then drop a short distance in order to begin flight.

If confronted with a bat problem, do not overreact. This very small, defenceless creature wants to escape as much as anyone could want him to leave. The best thing to do is put an empty wastebasket or box over the bat and call animal control or the nearest wildlife rehabilitation center. Often the little creature is exhausted from its attempts to escape, and a small fluid injection administered by the wildlife center will send it on its way to catch more insects.

If bats are living in an attic, roof, or house siding, and this is a problem, it is best to get professional advice from local wildlife people or animal control. One method used by experts to discourage bats from roosting in a building is to hang a piece of fine mesh or cloth over their entrance opening, attached only at the top, and at least twelve inches larger all the way around. In the evening the bats will be able to leave the roost, but they will be unable to return, so they will find a different roost site. The mesh can be removed in several weeks. This should not be done if the bats have non-flying young, however, because the young bats will die, which would be unfortunate enough in itself but would also create an odor problem. A rehabilitation center in the area may be able to tell you if young are present.

HOARY BAT
(*Lasiurus cinereus*)

The hoary bat is one of the largest of the Florida bats. Its brown coat is frosted with silver giving it a grizzled, hoary appearance. "Hoary" means having white or gray hair from old age, but the hoary bat has white-tipped hairs throughout its adult life. (The English word, cinereous, also means gray or ashy.)

This bat roosts in trees during the day, sometimes in clumps of Spanish moss, as do many other bats in Florida. It feeds at night on beetles, moths, and sometimes even smaller bats. Hoary bats roost individually, but mothers roost with their

△ Note the small, round ears.

young. When the babies become too heavy to carry, at about 4 to 5 weeks of age, they begin to fly on their own.

EVENING BAT
(*Nycticeius humeralis*)

Evening bats are fairly small and not nearly so brightly colored as the red, yellow, and Seminole bats. Their short fur is full and dark brown in color. They are rather nondescript in appearance and are often confused with other Florida dark-colored bats, such as the big brown bat and the southeastern bat. Evening bats are found throughout the Florida peninsula but, like most other bat species, are absent from the Florida Keys. They are one of the few bats that inhabits the Everglades.

Evening bat favor tree cavities for roosting, but they also roost behind loose bark. They rarely enter caves. They are most frequently encountered in Florida near stands of cypress. As the common name implies, the evening bat emerges from its daytime roost in the evening, well after dusk. This species migrates south in the winter, where numbers of them have been observed in South Florida roosting under palm fronds.

RAFINESQUE'S BIG-EARED BAT
(Plecotus rafinesquii)

As its name suggests, the most characteristic feature of this bat is its huge ears, which measure more than an inch in length. It also has two large lumps on its snout which give rise to the other common name of this species, the lump-nosed bat. Rafinesque's big-eared bat is a southeastern species found from the Dismal Swamp in Virginia south to Florida and west to Texas and Oklahoma. The big-eared bat is one of the rarest bats in Florida. It is most often caught in the northern half of the peninsula.

The size and shape of their ears help in identifying bats. Note the structure in the center of the ear of this Rafinesque's big-eared bat which is called a tragus. The tragus appears in many bats, but its function is not known. It has not been proven to play a role in the bat's hearing. Note the totally different shape of the ear and tragus in the photo of the hoary bat (page 20). When roosting, the extremely large ears are folded back along the body and under the wings, but if the bat is disturbed, the ears immediately become erect.

WAGNER'S MASTIFF BAT
(Eumops glaucinus)

The rare Wagner's mastiff bat is one of two free-tailed bats in Florida and the largest of the State's 16 bat species. At four to six inches in length and between one half and two ounces in weight, it is not really very big compared to most other mammals but is considered large for a bat.

This bat was once seen sporadically on Florida's southeastern coast, especially in the Miami area, but it has only been spotted twice since 1967. One of these sightings, however, involved the capture of a pregnant female in Coral Gables in 1988. This indicates that this species is not only still here but is breeding. However, it is so rare it is considered threatened in this state.

SOUTHEASTERN BAT
(Myotis austroriparius)

The southeastern bat, found in the northern half of the state, is one of the two most abundant species in Florida and is common in some areas. These bats give birth and rear their young primarily in caves. They have very specific temperature and humidity requirements and usually return to the same caves year after year. They prefer caves with water, and drowning is a major cause of death among the infants. Like other cave-dwelling species, this bat is declining in numbers because so many of its caves have been disturbed.

This species gives birth to twins. The mother's milk is extremely rich, richer than that of most mammals, and this allows her to wean her young in 3 to 4 weeks, a relatively short time. While she is nursing, the mother eats her own weight in insects every night.

Breeding colonies form in March, ranging from 2,000 to 90,000 pregnant females.

THE BAT BOMB

The roosting habits of bats once inspired an unusual plan to bring about an early end to World War II in the Pacific. The idea was to attach very light incendiary bombs to bats and release thousands of the armed creatures over Osaka, one of Japan's major industrial cities. The bats were expected to roost in the rafters of the buildings, which during that period were made mostly of wood. Timing devices would ignite all the firebombs at once, thus creating a vast firestorm.

*The feasibility of the plan was proven one day when a few of the bats in the United States escaped and burned down the control tower of the desert airbase where the project was located. Shortly thereafter, the idea was mysteriously abandoned by its Navy sponsors. There has been speculation that the project was derailed because of progress on the atomic bomb. A new book, **Bat Bomb**, by Jack Couffer, describes the operation in detail.*

Squirrels

GRAY SQUIRREL
(Sciurus carolinensis)

Gray squirrels are among the most common Florida mammals. They are found wherever there are trees, including parks and residential areas. Gray squirrels are found in densely wooded areas, but are also common in small wooded lots and back yards. In South Florida, they inhabit tropical hammocks and mangrove forests during the fruiting season. They avoid large clearings and rarely go more than a short distance beyond the forest's edge, because when they are out in the open, they are highly vulnerable to birds of prey and larger carnivorous mammals.

Gray squirrels eat whatever is seasonally available. Their main diet consists of acorns and nuts from late summer through the winter, but they also eat buds, fruits and berries, seeds, fungi, insects and insect larvae, and perhaps occasionally eggs or even a young bird. In Florida they are especially fond of acorns, pecans and hickory nuts, palm seeds, and pine seeds taken from pine cones.

In parts of the country where acorns are a primary food source, squirrel populations tend to follow the rhythm of the oaks. Oak trees have a several-year cycle from high to low acorn production, and squirrel populations rise and fall in step. A similar pattern has been confirmed in Florida for fox squirrels, and may hold true for the other Florida squirrel species as well.

Although they spend most of their lives in trees, gray squirrels often come to the ground to feed on mushrooms or fallen nuts and frequently hide nuts by burying them. This habit accounts for many of the trees that come up in yards and also natural areas.

SQUIRREL HIDE AND SEEK

Squirrels have several defenses against predators. They can freeze in an attempt to avoid notice or take cover in dens.

When no hiding place is available, they race to a tree and attempt to stay on the side of the tree opposite their enemies. Some birds of prey can overcome this defence by hunting cooperatively in pairs.

The squirrel in this photo has flattened its body against a tree to make itself less conspicuous.

△ Squirrel resting on a limb. Squirrels often flatten themselves against branches, possibly to make themselves less visible to predators. The tail is held over the back to provide shade in the summer and heat in the winter.

SQUIRREL TAILS

Squirrels' tails are covered with long, fairly stiff fur. Their tails have many uses. The gray squirrel's scientific name, Sciurus, comes from a Greek word meaning "shade," and indeed a squirrel often holds its tail over its back to provide shade on hot days. It also wraps its tail over its back to provide warmth on cold days. The tail can be used as an umbrella to keep off the rain. Another important function is to provide balance when the squirrel is running along branches, climbing, or engaged in other acrobatics. The flying squirrel uses its tail to help control its glide path. A variety of tail movements are used for communication when interacting with other squirrels.

Hunted in the past for food, gray squirrels remain a popular small game animal in Florida and are still used for food. In 1984-85, over 600,000 squirrels were taken by nearly 100,000 hunters. Both the squirrels and the hunters, however, are probably declining in numbers as the squirrels' favorite habitat continues to be lost to development.

During the Civil War and frontier days, gray squirrels were far more abundant than they are now. They were common robbers of camps and crops and were a staple food item themselves. Although they might threaten gardens, they do not threaten commercial farming today, in part because commercial seed is often treated with pesticides.

Gray squirrels are somewhat smaller in Florida than in more northern climates.

FLORIDA'S NATIVE SQUIRRELS

Gray squirrels are found throughout Florida, including the upper Keys. The other two native species, the southern flying squirrel and the fox squirrel, are everywhere in the state except the Keys.

Flying squirrels share the same habitats as gray squirrels. However, flying squirrels are active only at night, while gray squirrels are active during the day.

Fox squirrels are also generally active in daytime. Gray squirrels are smaller than fox squirrels and much more common in urban areas, as long as there are trees.

The chipmunk is also a member of the squirrel family. It is often overlooked as a Florida squirrel because it is rare in Florida (although common in northern states). It is only found in the northern parts of Florida such as Okaloosa County.

SQUIRREL NESTS

Gray squirrels nest in natural cavities in dead and dying trees or make nests of leaves on the limbs of trees. These leafy nests are especially visible in the winter when the foliage is sparse.

△ Gray squirrel carrying leaves to build nest.

△ Squirrel nest in winter.　△ Squirrel nest in summer.

SQUIRREL FUR

The gray color of the fur of the gray squirrel is usually the result of the visual mixing of several colors of fur, including brown, gray, and yellow outer hairs, and white and gray hair underneath. In addition, individual hairs have different bands of color from the tip to the base.

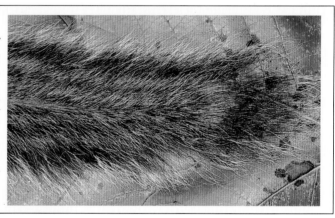

A SEEMINGLY UNNECESSARY TASK

Even where food is usually abundant in the winter, as in Florida, gray squirrels carry out all their food storage activities as eagerly as their relatives in the northern states. This means burying lots of acorns, storing food when it is abundant for the time when it is scarce. One reason for this seemingly unnecessary activity is that although there is a variety of food available throughout the year in Florida, not all foods have the same nutritional value as acorns. Acorns saved provide important calories during cooler weather.

BURIED TREASURE

Researchers have various theories about how squirrels keep track of their buried nuts. It is known that the buried treasure is shared by an entire community of squirrels. It had been thought that squirrels need not remember where they buried their nuts because they can locate buried nuts using their sense of smell. However, a recent study found that squirrels dig up a higher proportion of nuts they buried themselves than those buried by other squirrels, suggesting that memory may indeed be involved. Squirrels scatter their buried nuts over a wide area, perhaps to prevent other creatures that also eat nuts from uncovering a large cache. In city areas with little open land, squirrels often hide nuts in power transformers, leading to many squirrel electrocutions and some related power outages.

Squirrels

AN EXCITING CHASE

Squirrels are commonly seen chasing one another. Young fox and gray squirrels often engage in play-wrestling with their litter-mates, leaping onto tree trunks and running along branches to build strength and agility. But when adult squirrels are observed chasing each other, the chase often involves three or four males pursuing a female in heat. The males often stop to fight one another.

What appears to be a game is actually a serious matter of survival. The fittest male catches and mates with the female when she finally tires. This ritual insures that only the strongest males father the next generation of squirrels. It is difficult to breed squirrels in captivity because the chase is such an essential part of their mating activities.

Squirrels do not mate for life, and fathers have little to do with their families. After mating they go off to pursue other females. However, the chance that the first male to mate with a female will be the father of her litter is improved because, as a consequence of their mating, the female's vagina is blocked by a waxy plug which prevents other males from impregnating her. The plug is formed when a portion of the semen coagulates due to a chemical released from the prostate gland. The plug lasts about 24 hours and then drops out, but by then fertilization has likely occurred.

Although squirrel communities usually range over only a few acres or less, the males often travel over a wider area to find mates. This tendency helps prevent inbreeding and improves the species.

SQUIRRELS AND BIRD FEEDERS

Gray squirrels are noted for their ability to get into bird feeders, no matter how hard people try to keep them out. There have been contests for the best way to keep squirrels out of bird feeders, and entire books have been devoted to this subject, but the perfect feeder has not yet been invented.

Even if a bird feeder is suspended from a wire, far enough from branches so that squirrels cannot leap to the feeder, they can usually make their way to the feeder on the wire itself. If the wire is covered with PVC, however, the squirrels will fall off, because the PVC will rotate when they grab it.

Flying squirrels also get into bird feeders, but their piracy takes place at night, so it usually goes unnoticed.

▷ Squirrels have two postures for feeding : sitting on their hind feet, or hanging from their hind feet, head down.

▽ Children feeding squirrels should be warned that a squirrel may inflict a painful bite if allowed to approach too close. Squirrels grab and carry food with their mouths. Although generally not vicious, they may not distinguish between the food and the hand, especially if the hand smells like food.

SQUIRREL COLORS

There are places in the United States (such as Council Bluffs, Iowa) where gray squirrels with jet-black fur are rather common, but such melanistic squirrels are very rarely seen in Florida.

Florida does have gray squirrels that are white (albino) and beige (partial albinos), but these forms are not common. Gray squirrels in Florida vary somewhat from light to dark, but, in comparison to the highly variable color of fox squirrels, they seem to be mostly just gray.

◁ The hind legs of squirrels can rotate in their sockets to allow acrobatic postures such as the one shown in the photo at left and also the hanging feeding position shown at the top left of this page. This anatomy is unique among Florida mammals.

Squirrels

FOX SQUIRREL
(Sciurus niger)

These large, beautiful, generally solitary squirrels are found throughout Florida, except the Keys. Because they are far less common than gray squirrels and flying squirrels and usually live far from people, they are seldom seen. They are found in most types of forests within their range plus some suburban areas including golf courses and city parks.

Fox squirrels build platform nests in pines and hardwoods and stick nests in cypress. They also utilize cavities for nesting. They often nest in cabbage palms and in large clumps of bromeliads in other trees. In cypress trees, they often strip the bark to provide a soft inner lining for their nests. Such damage is a good indication of the presence of fox squirrels.

Not nearly as prolific as gray squirrels, fox squirrels are becoming increasingly rare throughout most of their range in the eastern United States. They have nearly vanished from the New England states, due to degradation and loss of the pine-oak forests they prefer, and their populations are declining in the southeastern United States for similar reasons.

△ Fox squirrels have unusually long tails.

A PERSISTENT MYTH

Some people believe that male fox squirrels bite the testicles off baby males to prevent them from becoming rivals. This story is not true. The source of the yarn may be the fact that squirrel testes remain in the abdomen until the young squirrels are about 10 months old, at which time they descend into the scrotum.

WHAT THEY EAT

Although fox squirrels are classified as tree squirrels (and are the largest tree squirrels in North America), they are actually semi-terrestrial. They nest in trees but usually forage for food on the ground, for which they need a fairly open understory. They eat seeds from pine and cypress cones, palm fruits, acorns, buds, nuts, and insects. They are especially fond of a particular mushroom which grows underneath slash pines. They hide fruits and nuts in holes in trees and in the ground. They may range over 50 acres in search of food, which varies seasonally and is sometimes scarce.

PROBLEMS WITH TAME SQUIRRELS

Fox squirrels are most commonly seen on golf courses and in state parks, where they often beg for food and generally make nuisances of themselves. They like to be handfed, but they become very bold if fed and may chew through expensive leather golf bags or do other damage to get to food. They easily become belligerent and sometimes bite. As with other wild animals, they should not be fed.

Squirrels

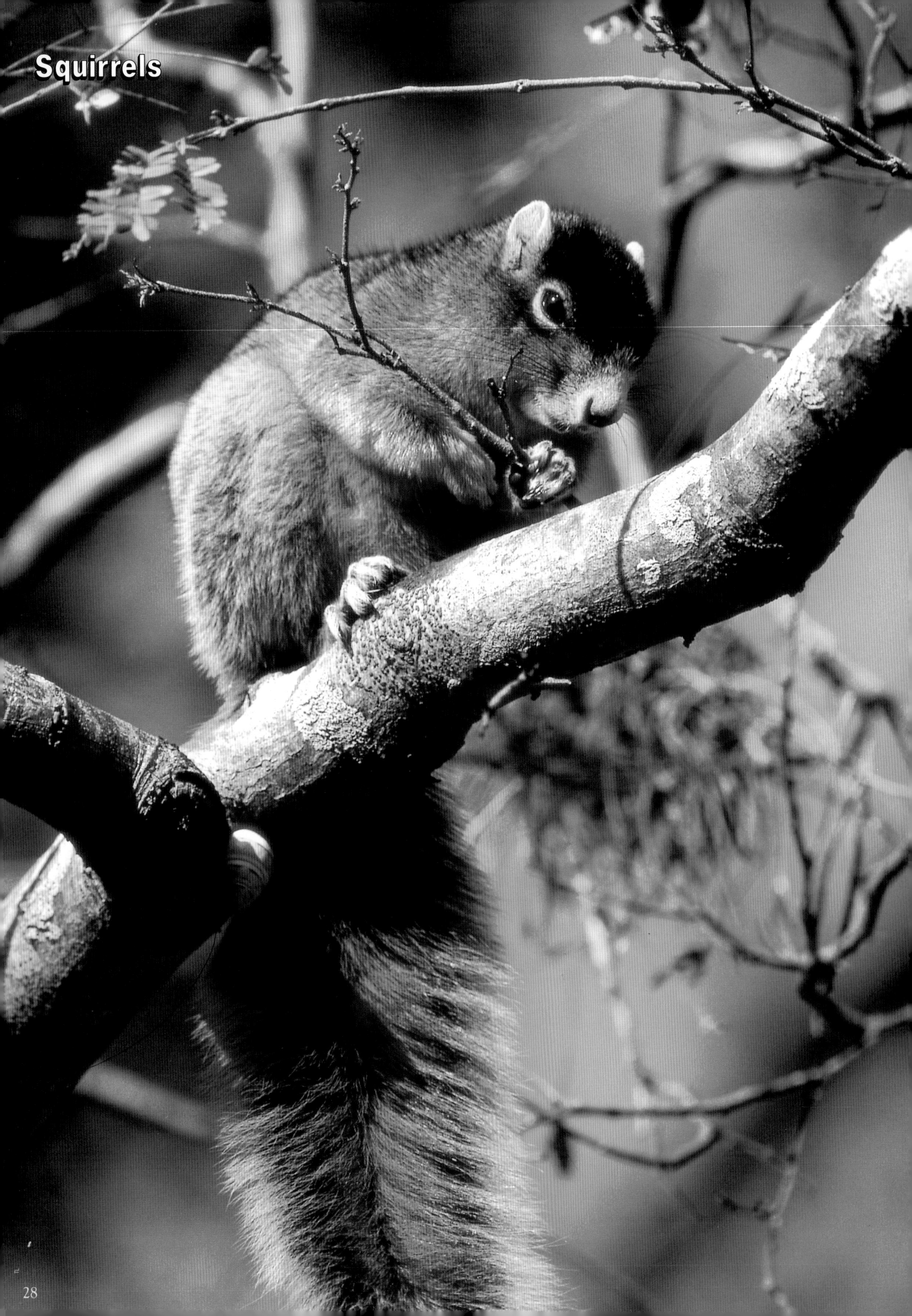

FOX SQUIRREL COLOR FORMS

Fox squirrels vary considerably in color even within the same colony (although this is not the distinguishing feature among the subspecies). The scientific name of the species (Sciurus niger) means black squirrel, and some fox squirrels are almost completely black, but most in Florida are gray and black or brown and black. Most fox squirrels have a black, masklike face with a white nose and white ears, and some have white feet. Fox squirrels sometimes look old because of their white-tipped (grizzled) hair. They are called monkey-faced squirrels by some people.

▽ Fox squirrels are twice as heavy as gray squirrels, sometimes over 2 pounds in weight.

FOX SQUIRREL SUBSPECIES

There are 3 different subspecies of fox squirrels in Florida and 10 in all of the United States. Sherman's fox squirrel is found throughout most of peninsular Florida. The Carolina fox squirrel is found in the Florida Panhandle and throughout the southeastern states. The mangrove fox squirrel, or Big Cypress fox squirrel, is found only in southwestern Florida. The subspecies are identified most easily by noting the part of the state in which they are found. Although there are a number of different color forms or phases, the same range of color is found within all the Florida subspecies, so color cannot be used to identify the subspecies.

Sherman's fox squirrel is found in isolated pockets throughout most of peninsular Florida. It likes to eat the seeds of the longleaf pine. Like other species of Florida squirrels, it is especially adapted to get at the seeds inside large, tough pine cones. Squirrels have strong incisors which act as powerful levers for opening pine cones and extracting the seeds. They also have strong, flat molars which are ideal for crushing the seeds. The favorite habitats of Sherman's fox squirrel include longleaf pine flatwoods and mixed forests of longleaf pine and turkey oak. The original habitat of this squirrel, longleaf pine in sandhill areas, has been reduced due to development. However, there is still a viable population of Sherman's fox squirrels living on the ranchlands of South-Central Florida.

Mangrove fox squirrels (another subspecies) are found primarily on pine islands in the Big Cypress Swamp area and the mangroves of southwestern Florida. Today they are officially listed as threatened, and hunting them is prohibited, although poaching is frequent. This subspecies is very rare and hardly ever seen, except on golf courses around Naples, where the squirrels are fed by golfers. Black individuals are more common within this subspecies. An orange and black form is especially beautiful.

SOUTHERN FLYING SQUIRREL
(*Glaucomys volans*)

The range and preferred habitats of the southern flying squirrel are basically the same as those of the gray squirrel, from oak hammocks to cypress swamps. If gray squirrels can be seen during the day, flying squirrels are probably in the same area at night. They are quite common in Florida.

Flying squirrels prefer to nest in natural tree cavities but sometimes build outside leaf-nests, like the other two squirrel species in Florida. Although they most often nest in cavities in live trees, they also utilize abandoned woodpecker holes or the abandoned nests of gray or fox squirrels in dead trees. They also occasionally make elaborate, multi-layered nests in Spanish moss, and they sometimes nest in electric boxes on highline wires, as do gray squirrels.

Flying squirrels usually maintain several nests, with fixed glide paths to these nests. If they are evicted from their main nest by larger animals, including gray squirrels, as sometimes happens, they move into one of their other nests. Like gray squirrels, they readily use bird houses as nest sites.

There are other species of flying squirrels in the United States such as the northern flying squirrel which is an important prey of the northern spotted owl.

RAIDING BIRD FEEDERS AT NIGHT

Flying squirrels come out about a half-hour after sunset. They make high-pitched squeaks or whistles as they chase one another in the dark. These sounds can often be recognized by someone familiar with their calls, but the flying squirrels are hardly ever seen because they remain hidden by the darkness. They frequently come to bird feeders at night, as do gray squirrels during the day, and they can be seen there if the feeder is illuminated with a red-filtered light. They spend very little time on the ground.

FLYING SQUIRRELS CANNOT REALLY FLY

Flying squirrels cannot really fly. Their "flight" is a gentle and graceful downward glide. When they spread their feet, a large flap of skin stretches between their front and rear legs on each side. Spread out, this skin looks like a parachute with a tiny body at the center. After launching themselves from the top of a tree, flying squirrels usually land on the trunk or branch of another tree 20 to 60 feet away. They then climb to the top, so they can jump and glide again to the next tree.

Flying squirrels leap from a head-down position high on the trunk of a tree, or from a horizontal limb, and then extend their legs to stretch their membrane taut. They usually glide up to about 60 feet. A "flight" of about 100 yards was once observed down an especially steep hill.

A flying squirrel holds its long tail over its back when it runs, but when it glides its tail is extended straight back and is used as a stabilizer and rudder. Flying squirrels have good control over the path of their "flights." They can make sharp turns, bank to avoid obstacles, and even execute downward spirals. The flight membrane is made of sheets of muscle. These muscles can be tensed or relaxed, so the glide can be controlled by varying the tension of the muscles as well as by moving the tail. When preparing to land, a flying squirrel swings its tail forward, causing its body to turn upward. This reduces speed and allows the squirrel to land face up against a tree trunk as shown below.

△ The arrows point to a strip of cartiledge which extends from the wrist to support and widen the flight membrane. Also note that compared to the gray squirrel which has a fluffy tail, the flying squirrel has a flat tail. The flatness of the tail makes it more useful as a rudder during glides.

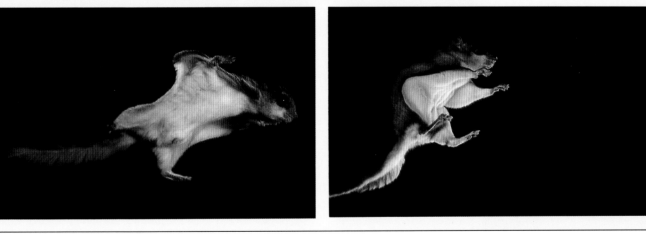

NUTS ABOUT NUTS

Nuts are their favorite food and acorns their staple, but flying squirrels also eat buds, seeds, berries, and mushrooms. They are among the most carnivorous of the squirrels and will eat insects, lizards, mice, and eggs. Like all squirrels, they also eat baby birds when the opportunity arises. They need lots of drinking water, so they usually live near streams or ponds.

Flying squirrels open nuts with their incisors, making a distinctive circular hole at one end; they use their long, lower incisors to scoop out the meat. They also use their front teeth like a hammer to wedge acorns and nuts into crevices for storage until winter. In cooler climates, in the fall, they may cache up to 300 nuts in a single night.

SOUTHERN FLYING SQUIRREL

The major predators of flying squirrels are owls. Whole colonies of flying squirrels may be completely wiped out by owls. Domestic cats also kill many flying squirrels and often deposit the tails on their owners' doorsteps. Other predators include bobcats, skunks, foxes, weasels, hawks, and occasionally snakes.

Flying squirrels are usually solitary in summer, but in the winter they live in colonies to keep warm, even in Florida. Several squirrels, usually four to eight but sometimes a many as 25, may crowd into a small cavity. During cold weather they become less active, but they become active again as the weather warms up. In colder states, they hibernate in winter. Squirrels from the same colony often "kiss" (touching their faces together as a greeting) when they meet, while strangers usually sniff rear ends, sometimes getting kicked in the face as a reward.

Young flying squirrels don't open their eyes until four weeks of age, and during this time the mother guards the nest well and leaves only briefly, because in addition to other predators, male flying squirrels may eat the babies and females may steal them. The pups begin to defend themselves at about five weeks and are weaned at about six weeks.

There are only two species of flying squirrels on this continent, but there are 30 species in Europe and Asia, the largest of which is 3 feet long. The Florida species is rather small, only 8 to 10 inches long, including its tail. It has large, black eyes and sleek, grayish brown fur, with a black fringe on the patagium, the name given the gliding membrane.

The southern flying squirrel ranges from southern Maine to southern Florida, excluding the Keys, and west to the edge of the Great Plains, with isolated pockets in Mexico and Central America. Ten subspecies have been identified, two of which are found in Florida.

FLYING SQUIRRELS AS PETS

Although most wild animals do not make good pets, flying squirrels have had some popularity. They were often kept as pets by the American colonists. They are sometimes sold by pet shops, even though they require state permits. Florida law now prohibits their capture, but they are still available. They are usually kept in a bird cage with cotton balls or stuffing which they can use to make a nest. They sleep all day, sometimes in people's pockets, and come to life when it gets dark. As house pets, they will jump from one person to another. They may live as long as 13 years in captivity, even though they seldom reach 5 years of age in the wild. On the down side, baby squirrels can grow up to be very rambunctious adults. Also, flying squirrels tend to get fat in captivity through overeating or inactivity, and may lose their ability to glide because their membrane cannot support their added weight.

EASTERN CHIPMUNK
(*Tamias striatus*)

The eastern chipmunk is extremely rare in Florida, although it is a very familiar animal further north and found throughout the eastern United States. It is not known how long chipmunks have been in Florida, but residents of Okaloosa County recall seeing them more than 60 years ago. Chipmunks live in the moist, hardwood forests of the Florida Panhandle, along river bottoms in Okaloosa County and a few neighboring counties.

Chipmunks spend nearly all their time on the ground, only occasionally climbing into trees, and even then not very high, although they are excellent climbers. They communicate with a little *chuck* noise and also make a variety of other sounds such as *chip*. They are diurnal, which means they are active only during the day. As dusk approaches they disappear into their burrows. They are generally solitary and somewhat skittish.

The adults are about two-thirds the size of gray squirrels and can easily be distinguished from other squirrels by the dark and light stripes running from their noses to the base of their tails. Compared to gray squirrels, chipmunks have shorter and less bushy tails. Their soft fine fur is reddish-brown in color and lighter on the underbelly.

They eat mostly seeds, berries, acorns, nuts, and fruits, but chipmunks also eat baby birds, mice, small snakes, frogs, slugs, insects, and occasionally mush-rooms. They sometimes make pests of themselves by munching on bulbs and blossoms in gardens. They have large internal cheek pouches, which open between the teeth and the lips, in which they carry food back to their burrows, where it is stored. When filled, these pouches cause the cheeks to bulge out enormously, giving the animals a rather comical appearance. The pouches are hairless, and the food they carry remains dry. The Latin name, *Tamias*, is a Greek word meaning "one who stores and looks after provisions," a reference to the cheek pouches.

Chipmunk burrows are lengthy and complex, up to 30 feet or more, with different chambers for nesting and food storage. The exit and entrance holes are often within a foot of one another. These are just open holes, with no evidence of excavated dirt around them. Eastern chipmunks are not true hibernators but they may sleep through a period of cold weather. Chipmunks are very vulnerable to predators, especially hawks and foxes. Their major underground predators are snakes and weasels, which can follow the chipmunk into its burrows, although weasels, like the chipmunks themselves, are rare in Florida.

In areas where there are human populations, domestic cats often greatly reduce the number of chipmunks.

△ The cheek pouches of this chipmunk are full of food which it is carrying to its burrow.

Pocket Gopher

SOUTHEASTERN POCKET GOPHER
(Geomys pinetis)

The Southeastern pocket gopher is commonly found in the northern two-thirds of Florida. This subterranean mammal is nicknamed "sandy-mounder," a reference to its habit of forming mounds of dirt in dry, sandy soil. (When Florida natives use the word gopher, they are generally referring to the gopher tortoise, a reptile.)

Pockets gophers are highly adapted for burrowing, with small eyes and ears but stout front legs and strong claws useful for digging. They tunnel with their eyes closed, pinching them shut so tight that sand and debris cannot get into them. They also close their lips behind their huge incisor teeth to keep sand out of their mouths. Their loose skin enables them to turn easily in their burrows. Their short hair aids in burrowing, as does their cylindrically-shaped body. Their sparsely-haired tail is touch-sensitive, which helps them know where they are going when they are moving backward in a tunnel.

Because pocket gophers plug their burrows completely, they require soil through which oxygen and carbon dioxide can pass freely in order to breathe. They tolerate higher levels of carbon dioxide and less oxygen in their atmosphere than most other mammals, including man, and this helps them survive in their tunnels. Still, they need a light, fairly loose, dry and sandy soil, and they avoid heavier soils that have poor gas exchange, such as certain clay soils.

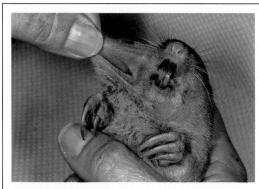

THE POCKETS

The cheek pouches of the pocket gopher are used for carrying food which will be stored in the burrow. Note that this is an external pouch (outside of the mouth and hair-lined), in contrast to the chipmunk, which has hairless pouches inside its mouth. The name pocket gopher comes from these pouches. The pouches, like pants pockets, can be turned inside out for cleaning or emptying. At one time it was believed that the pouches were used for carrying dirt, but any dirt found in the pouches is merely incidental.

◁ Its huge front feet and its long claws make it possible for the pocket gopher to dig very rapidly.

Most burrowing animals tend to have small ears and small eyes. This give them an advantage when digging through dirt.

Pocket gophers also have the ability (like nutrias and beavers) to close their lips behind their front teeth. This allows them to gnaw roots and dig through soil underground without getting dirt into their mouths (see photo in the nutria section, at the top of page 53).

Pocket gophers live apart from one another, each individual with its own territory. They only come together during the breeding season. A single gopher may make numerous mounds, up to one foot high and two feet across, often with no visible openings. There are usually far fewer animals in a given area than might appear from the mounds. The small tunnels beneath the mounds are packed with sand all the way back to the main tunnel to keep out snakes and other predators. The male's tunnel system is longer than that of the female, so the tunnels of one male may intersect the burrows of several females.

It is thought that pocket gophers get all the water they need from vegetation, so they don't need to drink. A pocket gopher kept in captivity for a number of weeks and never offered any water can maintain itself simply by eating stems, roots, flowers, and leaves. In the wild, they usually feed on roots and tubers just below the surface, but they may come out at night to forage for other vegetation.

Pocket gophers, like other mammals that burrow and live underground, have a relatively low rate of metabolism for a small mammal, especially when compared to shrews, which must eat their body weight daily. They cannot tolerate high temperatures for very long and will die if exposed to 100 degrees Fahrenheit for over an hour. The average gopher only lives a year, but a few may live as long as 5 years.

One of the predators of the pocket gopher is the pine snake, which spends considerable time hunting in pocket gopher tunnels. Pine snakes are able to find the mound openings and burrow through the plugs with their cone-shaped heads.

Today, pocket gophers are still considered pests by farmers and ranchers, and they have been controlled in the West and in the South through the use of poison baits. They become common if an area is over-grazed, and their activities tend to kill off the grass and vegetation or keep it sparse after the cattle are removed.

TUNNELING

Gophers dig extensive tunnel systems. A single tunnel can be from 20 to 500 feet in length, usually consisting of a main passage with short side tunnels branching off. Pocket gophers can turn around in their tunnels very rapidly if they need to flee.

Gophers dig two levels of tunnels. The upper level is usually a foot or so below the surface, and it is through these tunnels that the gopher finds its food, in the form of roots and other plant matter. It must continually dig new tunnels to maintain an adequate supply of food. A single pocket gopher excavates about one ton of soil per year.

Deeper tunnels can be from one and a half to five feet deep, with spiraling sections to connect the two levels. Pocket gophers dig the deeper tunnels for security. This is where they construct their nesting chamber for sleeping and raising their young.

A pocket gopher eats roots, tubers, and bulbs, and it tunnels in search of this food, whereas a mole uses its tunnels as pitfalls to catch insects and other food items. After consuming all available roots, a gopher digs new tunnels and abandons the old ones, which eventually collapse, while a mole usually maintains some of its tunnels for years. The gopher's mound is round, and the opening at the side is usually plugged with dirt. A mole's tunnel entrance is donut-shaped with an open hole in the center. Mole hills are less common in Florida due to the nature of the soil.

◁ A digging pocket gopher can really make the dirt fly!

▽ A typical sandy field full of the large mounds created by pocket gophers. Some people think these mounds are made by fire ants. The two may look similar after rain, but ordinarily the gopher mound is lumpier. A fire ant mound is not as high and is very smooth.

△ A trap is placed in a tunnel in order to catch pocket gophers for research.

△ These small mounds are not made by pocket gophers but by an insect, the scarab beetle. They often appear right next to the larger pocket gopher mounds.

THE BENEFITS OF TUNNELING

In the sandy soils found throughout most of Florida, nutrients are rapidly leached from the surface by rainwater percolating down through the soil. The burrowing activities of pocket gophers and gopher tortoises help maintain soil fertility by returning these leached nutrients to the surface. In a favorable habitat, pocket gophers may each year bring thousands of pounds of soil per acre to the surface as a result of their tunneling. Their bare mounds also serve as seed beds where young plants can become established. Unfortunately, these tireless efforts are rarely appreciated by people who seek to maintain immaculate lawns, pastures, and fairways.

BEAVER
(Castor canadensis)

Beavers are famous for their dam-building abilities, and their ability to fell trees is unique. By means of their dams, beavers alter their environment more than any other mammal besides man. (Elephants may also modify the land as much as beavers, according to some biologists.) The scientific name of the beaver's genus is *Castor*, a reference to their huge scent glands (see box, page 37), and their species is named *canadensis* because they were first encountered in Canada.

Beavers are the largest rodents of North America (north of Panama). The average beaver weighs 30 to 60 pounds. The largest beaver ever captured weighed 115 pounds. However, the world's largest rodent, the capybara of South America, is even larger than the beaver.

CUTTING TREES

Beavers use trees for both food and shelter. The inner bark of trees is their main food, but beavers will eat the succulent parts of many plants, avoiding the dry bark and the wood. To construct their lodges and dams, beavers cut down trees by chewing through the trunks. A beaver can fell a six-inch diameter tree in about 20 minutes.

Contrary to popular belief, beavers have no control over which way a tree falls. The tree simply falls toward the side they chewed the most. Most trees are probably chewed more on the downhill side, since that's the side the beaver encounters first when coming from the water, so it might appear that the beaver intends to have the tree fall toward the water.

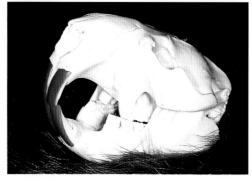

△ This beaver skull shows the large incisor teeth which grow throughout the animal's lifetime.

△ Beavers have split nails in the second toe of the hind feet which they use as combs. This is unusual, as most mammals groom with their teeth and tongue.

Beaver teeth are yellow-orange on the hard enamel front surface. The rear surface is soft (dentine) and wears fast, so their teeth are self-sharpening, a trait common to all rodents.

Like the incisor teeth of other rodents, the beaver's incisors continue to grow throughout its lifetime, up to several inches per year. They must spend a lot of time chewing to keep these teeth worn down to normal size. Pet gerbils, guinea pigs, rats, and mice, when fed a soft food diet in captivity, must have their teeth filed down periodically by a veterinarian.

Beavers have a transparent third eyelid which allows them to see underwater while protecting their corneas. Their ears and nose have valves so they can swim underwater without taking in water through these openings. Their exceptionally large liver stores a substance which releases oxygen when metabolized. This allows them to stay underwater for up to 15 minutes. However, they usually remain under only three to five minutes.

FLORIDA'S GIANT BEAVER

A giant beaver weighing several hundred pounds roamed through Florida thousands of years ago. Although long extinct, its fossils have been found here.

Beavers live in colonies of about five adults. They are basically nocturnal, but they can be seen in the late afternoon and early morning. Beavers build elaborate underwater lodges in northern states, but in Florida, most live in burrows dug into the banks of streams, although some do build lodges.

The major disease of the beaver is tularemia or rabbit fever, which can wipe out a whole colony at one time. People who drink unboiled water from a beaver pond will likely be exposed to this virulent and often fatal disease.

The beavers' dense fur has made them a favorite with trappers. The trapping of beavers was one of the major reasons for the opening of the West. The trappers were the very first people that pushed through to the West, seeking beavers for their valuable pelts. Wars were fought and fortunes won and lost over the trapping of beavers in North America. Their fur was so popular that beavers were nearly extinct throughout the United States and Canada by the end of the last century.

Beavers have come back into Florida in the past ten years, after having been wiped out by excess trapping, even though they receive no protection today. They're found mostly in the top tier of counties as far south as the Suwannee River. They are also found in the Santa Fe and Ichetucknee Rivers.

△ The broad beaver tail is used for steering in water or for slapping the water to signal alarm. It is also used as a prop to help beavers stand upright on land when they are gnawing on a tree. It may have a role in fat storage and body heat regulation.

The beaver is one of the few mammals that is monogamous, which means that the female will mate for life. Males will mate with more than one female, however. Beavers are very vocal, talking to each other constantly.

One male, one female, the current year's offspring, and several of the past year's offspring make up the family unit. The young may stay with their parents two to three years. Baby beavers (called kits) weigh less than a pound at birth and swim without urging before the end of their first day.

Beavers are easily preyed on by large carnivores and are easily trapped. Trappers use the oil from the castor glands of a beaver they have caught (not the same as castor oil obtained from plants and used as a medicine by people) as an attractant to lure other beavers.

Before Columbus there were as many as sixty million beavers in the United States. Each colony occupied about one-half to one mile of stream. They were found virtually everywhere.

PROBLEMS WITH BEAVERS

Beavers are admired by nature lovers but often hated by farmers, highway departments, and trout fishermen. Their dams often interfere with the activities of man, causing flowing water to back up, for example, and flooding farms. Beavers are often pests in northern Florida and are sometimes trapped or shot. Metal guards placed around valuable trees help to prevent damage.

FELT COWBOY HATS

Felt cowboy hats (made by Stetson and others) are stamped with a series of X's on the inside, indicating how many beaver pelts it took to make the hat. Felt is hair compacted under enormous pressure. The finer the hair, the more it can be compressed, and the higher the compression, the higher the quality of the felt and of the hat. The average cowboy hat ranges from one to four X's, meaning that hairs from one to four pelts were used to make the hat. 4-X hats can cost as much as $500. A rare 20-X hat could be worth $3,000. The felt hats that stimulated the beaver trade in the early days were elegant hats, not cowboy hats. Nowadays, most felt hats are made from compressed wool; very few are made from the fur of beavers.

SCENT GLANDS

The beaver is one of the very few mammals with a cloaca, an anatomical structure common among birds, reptiles, and amphibians. The cloaca is a chamber through which both the urine and the fecal material empty. In the case of the beaver, the scent glands also empty through the cloaca. Both male and female beavers have two sets of scent glands: anal glands and castor glands. Both of these glands are located near the tail, under the skin where they are not visible except as a bulge in very large individuals. These glands are similar to the anal glands of dogs and cats and the scent glands of skunks. Most carnivores have similar glands, but not as well developed. The beavers' scent glands produce a musk which they spread on trees and "scent posts," piles of sticks, mud, and grass about 12 inches in diameter, in order to alert other beaver colonies to their territorial claims. The odor can be noticed by humans at close range but is not as strong as the odor of a skunk.

COTTON MOUSE
(*Peromyscus gossypinus*)

The cotton mouse does not live in cotton fields as its name suggests, although in some areas it uses cotton from nearby fields as nesting material. This may be the origin of its common name. The scientific name, *gossypinus*, comes from a Latin word meaning cotton. This mouse likes to live in dense wooded timberlands and palmetto. It has been seen eating the seeds of sea oats on beaches, but that is not its preferred habitat.

Cotton mice are strong swimmers and great climbers. They nest in many places, in burrows, under logs, in the cavities around tree roots, in hollow trees, and occasionally in buildings.

The cotton mouse is found throughout Florida and is one of the most abundant mammals in Florida, but a rare subspecies found only on Key Largo was added to the federal endangered list about 10 years ago. The Key Largo cotton mouse is found in the same areas as the endangered Key Largo woodrat, including the Crocodile Lake National Wildlife Refuge and a few other uncut tropical hammocks remaining in northern Key Largo.

Like the Florida mouse, the cotton mouse has a distinct smell. It has six tubercles on each rear foot which helps to distinguish it from the Florida mouse, which only has five (see photo of tubercles on page 45).

△ Dueling cotton mice. This is a territorial battle between two males. Note the notches on the ears which are scars from previous fights.

FLORIDA NATIVE RATS AND MICE
Florida's native rats and mice are very beautiful little animals. There are several key identifying features for each species. These native rodents, unlike their introduced cousins, the house mouse, the black rat, and the Norway rat, are hardly ever household pests and should not be feared.

OLDFIELD MOUSE
(*Peromyscus polionotus*)

Oldfield mice inhabit the fields of abandoned farms, hence their name. They are also found in sandy habitats in central Florida. The subspecies found on the dunes and other sandy areas of beaches and barrier islands along the northern Gulf coast and Atlantic coast are called beach mice. Some subspecies of beach mice are so pale that they are almost white, whereas the oldfield mice living on darker soil in the inland areas are darker. Oldfield mice are smaller and have shorter tails than other Florida mice. Both beach mice and oldfield mice dig burrows in sand and build underground nest chambers. They come out mostly at night to feed on sea oats, other beach plants, and insects. They are rarely seen, but they leave mounds of dirt at the entrances to their burrows that can be as large as a pocket gopher's but are usually smaller. These native mice prefer natural habitats and do not invade homes.

△ The oldfield mouse is the lightest in color of all the native Florida mice and rats. Especially light-colored individuals, such as the one above, are sometimes called beach mice. The lighter-colored subspecies are usually found in beach habitats while the mice living on dark soil are usually darker. These variations in color which correspond to the habitats help to camouflage the mice and thus protect them from predators.

This species is, or was, a complex of at least eight subspecies, each found in fairly localized regions. Of the eight, only two are still fairly common in Florida today. Five of the subspecies are facing extinction, and one, the pallid beach mouse, has not been seen since 1946 and is presumed to be extinct.

Loss of habitat has been the primary cause of the near disappearance of these mice. As more and more houses and condominiums have been built along the coast, many of the dune systems where the mice formerly made their homes have been destroyed. Introduced mice and cats have also caused problems for oldfield mice. Outdoor domestic cats hunt the mice, and the non-native house mice which accompany people may compete with the native mice for food and living space. Tropical storms have also taken their toll.

The Perdido Key beach mouse is the most endangered of the five subspecies facing extinction. These mice are found only on one island just off the coast near the Florida-Alabama state line, in westernmost Florida. They were completely wiped out (extirpated) on the Florida portion of the island by Hurricane Frederick in 1979, and fewer than 100 individuals were counted on the Alabama side of the Key in 1987. They have since been reintroduced using individuals from the Alabama population. It seems that the mice have made a comeback and are becoming established in Florida once again. Nevertheless, mice from Alabama are still being released in Florida to increase the genetic diversity of the Florida population.

GOLDEN MOUSE
(Ochrotomys nuttalli)

Golden mice, along with cotton mice, are the only mice in Florida that live in trees (although cotton mice do not always nest in trees). Golden mice are found in a variety of habitats, from wet to dry, but always wooded, and usually with dense undergrowth. They range from central Florida north to Virginia and Illinois and west to Texas and Oklahoma.

These mice are semi-arboreal. They spend a good part of their life in bushes and trees, but they spend some time on the ground, too. The large tubercles or pads on both their front and hind feet aid in traction as they run through trees, up to 100 feet in the air. Their tail is capable of grasping. They use it for balance and sometimes even wrap it around twigs for support.

Their fur is a rich, golden color. Even the Latin name for the genus, *Ochrotomys*, means golden mouse (or, more precisely, ochre mouse). They have large, dark eyes and big ears. Fortunately for them, these adorable creatures are seldom seen, even by experienced nature lovers, because of their secretive, nocturnal habits.

Golden mice build their own nests or modify birds' nests. These nests are sometimes on the ground but more often from a few inches to 15 feet above the ground, in trees or shrubs, usually hanging amidst Spanish moss or in vines. The nests are oval in shape and have a coarse outer layer but are lined with softer materials, fur, feathers, or vegetation, which the mice fluff up with their

teeth. The round nests, 3 to 12 inches in diameter, may be used year after year.

Golden mice are highly social animals. They live in small communities, like extended families, consisting of 3 to 4 nests, with up to 8 mice per nest. A community of golden mice generally forages over a relatively small area, about one acre in size.

The males leave the nests when the blind, deaf, and hairless young are born. The young mice are quite vulnerable in the nest, but they develop relatively quickly and are weaned at around 3 weeks of age. The mother may become pregnant again while nursing and have as many as 8 litters a year in the wild, but 2 to 3 litters per year would be normal.

Golden mice eat fruits, acorns, and many other kinds of seeds, but insect and other invertebrates are also a substantial part of their diet. They often carry seeds to their feeding platforms in their internal cheek pouches. These feeding platforms, which resemble the nests, may be shared by neighboring communities.

Although they may live as long as 8 years in captivity, their average life span in the wild is probably no more than 6 months. They are preyed upon by owls, hawks, foxes, bobcats, skunks, and snakes. They are slower than squirrels and cannot escape predators by running, so their usual defense is to freeze when threatened and lie flat against a limb. On the ground, they tend to move slowly and freeze often.

Quite a bit is known about these mice, compared to most of Florida's small rodents, because they have been tagged and studied at the Archbold Biological Station near Lake Placid, Florida. They are trapped using a bait made of peanut butter, oatmeal, and raisins. A numbered tag is attached to one ear before a newly trapped mouse is released. Recapture of these tagged mice has increased our knowledge of their territories and habits.

◁ The golden mouse is the only native Florida mouse which feeds and sleeps in trees. Among the non-natives, the black rat also spends much of its time in trees.

RATS VERSUS MICE

Scientists seldom make a distinction between rats and mice although non-scientists often use the two names to distinguish between large and small rodents. Rats are generally larger than mice, but rats and mice are both rodents, and they share too many overlapping features to make a clear distinction between them. This problem is similar to comparing toads and frogs. Both are amphibians with many overlapping characteristics.

FLORIDA MOUSE
(Podomys floridanus)

This mouse is unique to Florida. It is found nowhere else, and its closest relatives live in central Mexico. These are the largest of Florida's mice, weighing up to 40 grams or more. They have large black eyes, big ears, and large rear feet. The 5 tubercles on each hind foot, pads which look like lumps of tough skin, are helpful for identification and are used for traction (the same as those of the cotton mouse). Florida mice are also called gopher mice, because they prefer to live in gopher tortoise burrows, although they use pocket gopher tunnels and other kinds of burrows as well. They are found in dry scrub or woodland habitats and eat insects and seeds.

Florida mice have a distinct, skunk-like smell. Individuals of some populations are very tame when handled. In Florida, this mouse most closely resembles the cotton mouse.

The Florida mouse is a threatened species because of its small geographic range and the destruction of its habitat by development. They are found in scattered populations on the Florida peninsula only as far south as Highlands County, but not in the Panhandle (except one isolated population at Carabelle) nor the Keys.

△ The Florida mouse is known for its huge ears.

EASTERN HARVEST MOUSE
(Reithrodontomys humulis)

The Eastern harvest mouse resembles a house mouse, but it is the only mouse in Florida with grooved upper incisors. It is uncommon in Florida. It likes waste fields of grass, wet bottom land, flatwoods, pastureland, and prairies. It nests in grasses above the ground. The Eastern harvest mouse doesn't make runways but may use the passageways of the cotton rat. It sometimes stores seeds.

MICE AS PREY

Most small mammals are nocturnal in habit and are almost never seen. As a result, they are often overlooked, yet they play an important role in maintaining plant and animal communities. Small mammals provide an abundant source of food for meat-eating mammals, birds, and snakes. The barn owl, a medium-sized owl, preys almost exclusively on small rodents.

△ A barn owl carrying its most common prey, the hispid cotton rat.

EASTERN WOODRAT
(*Neotoma floridana*)

Sometimes known as a pack rat, this large rodent belongs to the same genus as the true western pack rats. Like the other rats to which it is most closely related, it uses a variety of natural and man-made items in the construction of its houses, although they are primarily made of sticks. The Eastern woodrat is found in hardwood hammocks and other forest habitats.

When not breeding, woodrats are aggressive, continually fighting and chasing one another. Adults are commonly scarred from these battles, with their ears torn or part of the tail missing. These rats have many predators, including birds of prey, rattlesnakes, and many other snakes.

The Eastern woodrat is completely vegetarian, with a varied diet of fruits, berries, and other plant parts. It is not an economic pest. Woodrats are very large rats, from one to two pounds for a large male, and at one time they were considered by some people in the Old West, probably hungry people, to be good eating.

Woodrats do not breed as fast as most other rats. They do not start breeding until they are seven or eight months old and have only two or three small litters per year.

Woodrats forage on the ground as well as in trees.

There is only one species of woodrat in the Eastern United States, but there are several species of woodrats in the western part of the country.

△ Although similar in size, the woodrat can be distinguished from the introduced Norway rat by its large, round ears, long white or black whiskers, and white feet and belly. The woodrat also has a distinctive, hairy tail which is dark above and light underneath.

THE WOODRAT NEST

Its large nest looks like a pile of sticks and might contain almost anything, including items collected from around homes and trash cans. The woodrat lugs all sorts of items to its nest in addition to sticks, including leaves, cloth, bones, shotgun shells, and items from campsites. It sleeps in a safe spot in a separate cavity or tunnel. The nests are built in hollow trees or over holes in the ground in low, wet areas. These nests are waterproof and, due to their bulk, afford good protection against owls and most other animals. If they are invaded, it is only by snakes and small mammals.

One peculiar characteristic of these rats is that they do not defecate in their nests. They share common "poop piles," or latrines, located outside but nearby the nest. These piles may contain several quarts of excrement. The telltale piles reveal that woodrats live nearby.

△ ▷ Above is a woodrat nest built in an old, abandoned automobile. At right is the massive pile of materials that makes up a woodrat nest in the wild.

KEY LARGO WOODRAT
(*Neotoma floridana smalli*)

Considered a subspecies or race of the Eastern woodrat, the Key Largo woodrat is found on less than 2,000 acres of northern Key Largo. This rat has habits similar to the Eastern woodrat but is isolated from the other woodrat populations in Florida, which are found no further south than Lake Okeechobee.

These cute animals, with their soft, dense fur and large, round eyes and ears, were added to the United States endangered list about ten years ago because the habitat in which they survive had been largely destroyed. These woodrats prefer mature tropical hardwood hammocks where they feed on leaves, buds, fruit, and seeds high in the trees. They sometimes build stick nests in trees, where they are protected from ground predators, but they also build ground nests shaped like beaver lodges or nest in holes among tree roots or cracks in the limestone soil.

The tropical hardwood hammocks in which the Key Largo woodrat is found were never very extensive in Florida, and most have been destroyed as a result of development. This uncommon habitat is home to a large number of plants and animals, many of which have been listed as threatened or endangered.

HISPID COTTON RAT
(*Sigmodon hispidus*)

Along with the cotton mouse, this is one of the most common native small mammals in Florida and certainly the most common rodent in the southeastern United States.

The hispid cotton rat is not found in buildings. It spends its entire life outdoors, and it is often the most abundant species on southern farms, where it is now considered a major pest of crops. It can cause a 50% loss in sugar cane by severing the stalks close to the ground. It is especially fond of sweet potatoes and is attracted from long distances by a field of them.

The cotton rat, unlike the nocturnal rice rat, feeds both day and night if in dense cover. It eats mostly seeds and green vegetation, especially grass. Predominantly a land mammal, it doesn't swim much compared to the rice rat. This small rat, which has a somewhat grizzled appearance (to which the name hispid refers).

The hispid cotton rat is the most prolific of all rodents in Florida. Because of this, it is a ready food source for bobcats, owls, and many other predators. The young leave the nest quickly, only 5 or 6 days after birth.

MARSH RICE RAT
(*Oryzomys palustris*)

This common rat lives primarily in a variety of wetland habitats, including salt and fresh water marshes, and it is common around flooded fields. It is a source of food for owls, hawks, foxes, skunks, weasels, mink, and especially water moccasins and other water snakes.

A truly amphibious rat, the rice rat is very much at home in the water, on the surface or beneath. It swims and dives readily, and it is a good swimmer, attaining speeds approaching two feet per second.

The rice rat also makes tunnels through marsh grasses and burrows underground. In certain habitats, it is probably the most common of all rats.

This omnivorous rat is nocturnal; it only feeds at night. It eats seeds and fruits primarily, but also insects, and even small crustaceans and fish. When rice paddies were common in Florida, the rice rat would feed on the rice at various stages in its growth, including fallen rice after the harvest.

The marsh rice rat constructs feeding platforms by bending vegetation. It makes woven grassy nests in tangled vegetation, usually in a slight depression in the ground, but sometimes as much as a meter above the ground in marshy areas.

MORE RODENTS THAN...

In numbers of species and of individuals, rodents outnumber all other mammals. Nearly 50% of the approximately 4,000 mammal species in the world are rodents (another 22% to 25% are bats). Rodents play a major role in many ecosystems, and yet we know relatively little about them.

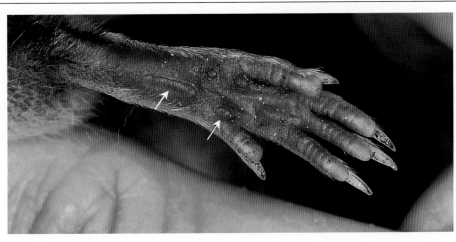

FOOT PADS

The length of the hind foot and the pattern of tubercles (pads) on the foot are both used to identify species of rats and mice whose color, size, and tooth patterns are so similar that the animals cannot be easily distinguished. Although this photo of a rice rat foot is used as an example, the tubercle pattern is most useful for identification of the cotton mouse and the Florida mouse.

KEY RICE RAT
(*Oryzomys argentatus*)

This rare rodent makes its home in marshes, fields and mangrove swamps in the lower Florida Keys, primarily Cudjoe Key. It is found only in small numbers and has a limited distribution. Therefore, it is perhaps not surprising that it is the most recently described mammal species of the eastern United States. There is some disagreement among mammalogists whether this rat should be considered a distinct species or a subspecies of the marsh rice rat. The state of Florida lists it as a species, but one recent study of rodent skulls indicates that it is more likely a subspecies.

The most distinctive feature of the lower Keys rice rat is its color which is brownish-gray on the back with silver-gray at the sides. It is also called the silver rice rat because of this color (argentatus means silver-colored). Most other rice rats are brown. Scientists rely on the shape of its nasal bones for accurate identification.

ROUND-TAILED MUSKRAT
(*Neofiber alleni*)

Smaller than the common muskrat of the North and Midwest, this muskrat is not trapped for its fur, although it has a good, dense fur. It is actually a large vole, although it has been called the Florida water rat. It is an excellent swimmer and takes to water readily. It is nocturnal. Like its name implies, its tail really is round. True muskrats from the North have vertically flattened tails.

Round-tailed muskrats make small, dome-shaped houses from marsh grasses thatched tightly together. Each house has a floor or platform just above the water line, called a diving platform, with two holes at opposite ends of the platform. The round-tailed muskrat sits on this platform, and if threatened by an animal that comes up one of the holes or through the top of the nest, it dives down the other hole.

Barn owls are especially fond of round-tailed muskrats. Marsh hawks and water moccasins also feed on them as well as dogs, cats, and alligators.

The round-tailed muskrat is almost as restricted in its range as the Florida mouse and is only found in Florida and Georgia.

FEEDING PLATFORMS

Most animals eat food wherever they find it, in fields or ponds for example, but some rodents, such as the nutria, beaver, muskrat, and some mice, drag their food back to a place which is relatively secure from predators before starting to eat. Often, the safest location is over water. Platforms made of sticks or grasses provide an elevated view of predators and also keep the food out of the water.

Muskrats build feeding platforms of fine grasses near their houses, just above the water. These feeding platforms afford some protection from predators and also provide the muskrats with a better view of the surroundings. From these platforms, the muskrats feed on succulent grasses and other aquatic plants from the surrounding area.

△ The home of the round-tailed muskrat consists of grass thatching. The roof has been torn off this home to reveal the two plunge holes, one on each side, which are used to escape predators

Round-tailed muskrats sometimes live in burrows rather than grass houses. If the water level of their pond drops substantially, these rodents will burrow into the soil in the banks or bottoms of the pond and have their young there.

◁ Maidencane grass is a principal food of the round-tailed muskrat.

Voles

MEADOW VOLE
(*Microtus pennsylvanicus*)

The primary range of meadow voles, sometimes called field mice, is in the northeastern United States and in the Midwest. In Florida they are extremely rare, found only in the salt marshes of Levy County, along the Gulf Coast south of Florida's "Big Bend" region, near Cedar Key. These Florida voles were not discovered until 1982! They are a subspecies of the meadow vole called the saltmarsh vole. In other parts of the country, meadow voles are among the most prolific of all mammals. However, very little is known about the Florida population.

Meadow voles eat vegetation such as grasses, seeds, fleshy rootstocks, and tender bark. In other parts of the country they cause some crop damage, but that is not the case in Florida since their numbers are so few. In spite of repeated trapping efforts, only a single vole has been captured in the past 13 years.

In the Northeast and Midwest, where meadow voles are numerous, they provide predatory birds and mammals with an abundant source of food. They are preyed upon by many species of animals.

Voles resemble stocky mice, but they are more closely related to muskrats and lemmings. This group of animals has a stocky build, short tail, small ears, and different teeth, compared to mice.

△ This photo shows the grassy nest of the meadow vole, while the top photo shows the vole sitting up in its nest.

△ All voles have small ears. Their Latin name *Microtus* comes from *micro otis*, meaning small ear.

RUNWAYS AND RACEWAYS
Runways are paths through undergrowth which serve somewhat like highways for small creatures. They are like above-ground tunnels through brush and tall grasses.

PINE VOLE
(*Microtus pinetorum*)

Also called the pine mouse, the pine vole is common in some areas of the Panhandle, but rare in Central Florida. It is seldom found in pure stands of pines, so its common name is somewhat of a misnomer, but it will occupy mixed hardwood-pine habitat.

Basically "fossorial" or burrowing creatures, pine voles live in leaves, with their burrows and nests just below the leafy layer of the soil. These small rodents seldom venture any distance above ground, except to scamper over the surface into another burrow.

Pine voles eat shrubs, grasses, roots, tubers, stems, peanuts, potatoes, and other vegetable crops. They are also cannibalistic. Pine voles are smaller and darker in color than meadow voles.

NORWAY RAT
(*Rattus norvegicus*)

The Norway rat is the larger of the two Old World rats in Florida . Compared to the black rat, its tail is shorter. The Norway rat is rather scarce in Florida, although it can be seen around granaries and in the salt marshes along the Atlantic coast.

The Norway rat is especially known for feeding on stored food. The Norway rat can puncture tin cans to get at food in the home, and it will eat soap, meat, vegetables, poultry, and especially grain. Much more food is contaminated with the rats' fecal matter and urine than what the rats themselves consume. Such food cannot be cleansed and must be destroyed.

△ Note the short tail (shorter than the body) which distinguishes this Norway rat from the black rat.

THE GOOD NAME OF RATS

The activities of the few pestilent species of the genus Rattus have adversely affected the reputation of all mammals with the word rat in their common names. However, most of the economic and health problems caused by rats in Florida are associated with only two species.

The black rat is found throughout the world and is responsible for the spread of disease and great agricultural losses. The Norway rat, known over most of the world for its destruction of property and stored food, is a threat to the safety of people, domesticated animals, and wildlife. Under certain conditions several other species of rats have become pests in local areas.

BUBONIC PLAGUE

Plague is a worldwide problem, not just limited to Europe. Historically, outbreaks have been divided into several major time periods. We are currently in the fourth outbreak, which began in Yunan, China in 1860. In India there were 10 million plague victims between 1900 and 1950. In the early part of this century, serious outbreaks in the United States occurred in San Francisco, Galveston, and New Orleans. There are currently less than 100 plague victims every year in the U.S., mostly in the southwestern states. The invention of streptomycin in 1948 greatly reduced the death rate among plague victims.

The disease reaches man through bites from infected fleas carried by rats, and not directly from the rats. Rats carry fleas which carry the bacteria which causes the plague (also called the black death). When a plague-infected rat dies, the fleas carrying the bacteria move to another animal or to man.

OLD WORLD (EUROPEAN) RATS IN AMERICA

The rats and mice which were inadvertently brought to the Americas from Europe are the black rat, the Norway rat, and the house mouse. These are the rats and mice that people most often encounter because of their tendency to live in human dwellings. The generally harmless native rats and mice are much less frequently seen because they prefer to live in natural habitats. So when people think of rats and mice, unfortunately, it is usually the harmful exotic species which come to mind.

CLEAN RATS?

Rats are considered dirty, but they spend a good part of each day grooming themselves. After eating in some filthy place such as a garbage can, they clean themselves. Notice that the Norway rat above has taken its whiskers into its mouth for cleaning. Rats spread disease through their droppings, which wind up in grain and in human food. Thus, rats are very unsanitary, but they are not unclean. In fact, if a human touches a mouse or rat, the rodent will immediately proceed to clean itself vigorously.

BLACK RAT
(Rattus rattus)

The black rat is the most abundant of the introduced rats in Florida. It is common in palm trees where it makes nests in the thatch. It can easily be seen at night eating the palm fruits. It is often found around seawalls and is sometimes called water rat. It is also called attic rat or roof rat because it is frequently found in attics. This rat is the animal that carries bubonic plague. It is also of major importance in carrying the infectious agents of other diseases such as typhus. Wherever black rats are found, public health officials have to be alert to the possibility of epidemics of rat-borne diseases.

BLACK RAT VS NORWAY RAT

Although the black rat is by far the more common and widespread of the two species in the tropics, the Norway rat has proved to be more adaptable in cooler places, especially in cities. As the Norway rat spread through North America and Europe, it drove the black rat from its favored habitat on the ground and the lower levels of buildings. Thus, the black rat has become rare in many areas and has even been designated as endangered in the state of Virginia (which is a bit strange because endangered status is used to give protection to a native species— public health officials no doubt wish that they could make this rat endangered throughout the United States).

△ Damage from the black rat shows why this rodent is also called the roof rat.

CONTROLLING RATS

Poison only works for the period it is used. As soon as the poison is no longer supplied, the population will spring back. Cats are an ancient deterrent, but cats can only kill a limited number of rats. Although the average rat lives no more than a year, rat populations can quickly multiply to match the size of the available food source. Rats can be permanently eradicated only by eliminating garbage and carelessly stored food supplies, and the environmental conditions that provide suitable shelter for the animals.

◁ The tail of this black rat is longer than its body. The tail of the Norway rat is shorter than its body. This is the best way to distinguish the two species.

▽ The tails of this black rat (and also the Norway rat) appear hairless at first glance but actually have sparse, short hairs. However, their tails are more naked than those of the native Florida rodents.

Rice Rat

Black Rat

◁ These skulls show how different the tooth patterns of rodents can be. These differences are very valuable for identification. The teeth of the black rat have three cusps while those of the native rice rat have only two. In both cases the cusps aid in crushing seeds and other food.

HOUSE MOUSE
(*Mus musculus*)

This mouse sometimes takes up residence in grassy fields in wastelands and also colonizes the cabbage palm thickets along Florida's west coast, but it mostly inhabits buildings or other areas in close association with human dwellings. It may be confused with certain forms of the harvest mouse, from which it differs in size, coloration, and by the absence of grooves in its upper incisors.

The house mouse is to a great degree a nomadic species when living outdoors. Indoors, the persistent chewing on partitions and little black pellets on the pantry shelf are often the only signs of the presence of this tiny beast. Although a single individual will not pilfer any great quantities of food in one night, the combined depredation of several dozen over a few months time may be considerable.

Unfortunately, these mice, like their larger cousins, the Norway and black rats, are very prolific. It's not unusual for them to produce a litter of 10 or 11 young, although the usual number is 5 to 7. They have various songs, squeaks, and calls. The successful establishment of this species over the entire world is perhaps due to its fortitude and endurance as much as its adaptability. They are known to be able to survive longer periods of captivity in traps than many other species and are generally very hardy.

△ The house mouse has a very long tail and, unlike native Florida mice, seems to prosper in man-made structures. Any mouse found in a human dwelling is most likely a house mouse.

◁ The house mouse is not as serious a pest as the black rat and the Norway rat, but it can contribute to the spread of such diseases as food poisoning, murine typhus, and the plague, and it is often an agricultural pest. It consumes some stored human food and contaminates far more. It also destroys woodwork, furniture, upholstery, and clothing.

THE BAD RAT

The harmfulness of rats to man is unmatched in the mammal world. Rats are thought to eat about one-fifth of the world's crops each year. Norway and black rats consume vast quantities of food and grains and contaminate much more than they eat. They also chew on electrical wires, sometimes starting fires. On a worldwide basis, the direct damage caused each year by these two species amounts to billions of dollars. Rats also spread some 40 different diseases. They carry the black death or bubonic plague which killed about one-quarter of the population in medieval Europe. Bubonic plague is still a threat in many parts of the world. It is estimated that rat-borne diseases have taken more lives in the past 1,000 years than all the wars ever fought. Furthermore, rats frequently bite people. Over 10,000 rat bites are recorded every year in the U.S. alone. Yet rats are hard to control. Not only are they highly adaptable, but they are among the most prolific mammals on earth. A single pair of rats can have (under ideal conditions) up to 15,000 descendants in one year.

THE GOOD RAT

On the plus side, rats contribute more to medical research than any other mammal. The common laboratory rat used all over the world is a white mutant version of the Norway rat. The house mouse is also used. Nearly all new drugs are tested on these lab animals.

△◁ The laboratory mouse above is an albino version of the house mouse. At left is a breeding facility for laboratory mice.

Rats are often admired for their survivorship. They are probably the most numerous mammals on earth and, with the possible exception of man, the most successful.

WHAT IS A RODENT?

The one feature that distinguishes the rodents is their chisel-like front teeth, one pair in the upper jaw and one pair in the lower jaw. These teeth continue to grow from their base throughout the life of the animal. The word "rodent" comes from the Latin word "rodere" meaning "to gnaw." As rodents gnaw, their ever-growing teeth are worn down. The rear surface of the teeth consists of soft dentine which wears faster than the hard enamel on the front of the teeth. This unequal wear maintains the sharpness and the chisel-like shape of the teeth. This adaptation, along with a very high reproductive rate, has helped rodents become a very large and successful group of mammals, and enabled them to exist in a wide variety of habitats. They range in size from a tiny mouse to the capybara which can weigh a hundred pounds.

WHY DO SOME MAMMAL TESTES HANG DOWN?

Most design features of mammal bodies can be explained as evolutionary adaptations that gave the animal a greater chance of survival and were thus reinforced through natural selection and the survival of the fittest. However, why do the testes of most mammals hang outside their bodies in a pouch, the scrotum, in a position that makes the delicate organs painfully vulnerable to a bite or a swift kick?

The reason is not fully understood. After all, the testes of shrews, elephants, and whales are tucked up safely inside their bodies, seemingly a more practical design.

According to one theory, testes hanging a slight distance away from the body cavity allow sperm to remain a few degrees cooler and thus more active and more viable.

WHISKERS

Whiskers (called vibrissae in technical language) are sensory organs for touch. They are extremely long in rodents. Rodents are nocturnal and must go through small spaces where the extra touch sense helps them navigate in the dark. The domestic cat also has outstanding whiskers. Some animals have whiskers not just on the usual place, the cheeks, but also above the eyes, on the chin, etc.

TAILS

Tails can be classified as grasping or non-grasping. An example of a grasping tail is that of the opossum which uses its tail to assist in climbing. Although some monkeys are well known for their grasping tails, the tails of most Florida animals cannot grasp. Some animals, such as the bear, have almost no tail.

Animals use their tails for a variety of purposes. For example, the Florida panther uses its tail for balance when running (for tight cornering). Foxes and squirrels wrap their tails over their bodies to stay warm. Squirrels also use their tails as shade in order to stay cool in summer. Squirrels shake their tails when angry as a threat gesture. They may even shake them in time with their scolding voice in order to reinforce their voice. This may help to startle a marauding bird or another competitive squirrel. Beavers use their tails to slap the water for communication. The White-tailed Deer raises its tail to reveal a white spot which alerts the rest of the herd to danger. The spotted skunk uses its tail for balance when standing on its front feet to spray. Marine mammals use their wide, flat tails for propulsion.

CAPTURE-MARK-RECAPTURE

Many wild animals have been studied using a technique called capture-mark-recapture. The animals are caught in live traps using bait, then marked with numbered tags in their ears or by other means, and released. Each time they are caught again, something is learned about their range and their habits.

Obviously, this technique only works with animals that are caught fairly readily and do not quickly become wary of the traps. In the case of animals that are difficult and that must be chased, radio tracking is used to monitor their whereabouts and in that way learn more about their behavior. Radio tracking has been used with panthers, manatees, gray foxes, and other species as well.

EFFECTS OF FEEDING WILDLIFE

Although it may be helpful in times of natural disaster or for animals facing the threat of extinction, the feeding of wild animals by humans usually has negative effects on the animals. Such feeding upsets natural balances and can artificially inflate the size of populations such as raccoons, squirrels, and deer far beyond the carrying capacity of the land. Thus, there would be artificial die-offs when the feeding is stopped. In addition, abnormally large population levels are often associated with more parasites and infectious diseases, because of crowding and stress. This can weaken the entire population. Finally, feeding usually reduces the wild animals' normal and very healthy fear of man.

THE DECLINE OF HUNTING

Hunting has been an American tradition since the time of the colonists. In addition to procuring food, hunters matched their wits against animals for sport. Sons proudly accompanied their fathers on the opening day of the annual hunting season. But today, hunting is going the way of the open range and the steam engine. Relatively few teenagers in rural areas show any interest in hunting. Guns have become associated with self-defense. Hunting regulations have become complex and very restrictive. Many private landowners have shut out hunters for fear of litigation. Nuisance animals are now humanely trapped and relocated. The irony is that although small game is decreasing due to loss of habitat, deer and hog, the most popular large game animals in Florida, are present in larger numbers than ever before.

△ Rural Floridian hunters pose proudly with their wild hog.

NUTRIA
(Myocastor coypus)

The nutria looks somewhat like a cross between a common northern muskrat and a beaver. It has a mouth with a muscular rim which closes tightly behind the teeth, thus allowing it to carry things in its mouth while swimming without taking in water. Its incisors are curved and distinctively orange-red in color. Nutrias generally prefer fresh water but are also found in brackish and salt water. They are primarily nocturnal.

The species name *coypus* is Indian in origin and translates as "water sweeper." Nutria is a Spanish word for otter, but the web-footed nutria is a rodent and is not related to otters.

The nutria's incisor teeth, like those of the beaver and other rodents, have no root but are formed in a continuous manner from the adjoining tissue. This allows them to continue growing throughout the animal's lifetime. This is an adaptation for feeding on tough vegetation which wears the teeth down.

Nutrias were originally introduced in 1899 into the United States from South America, where they are native, for fur farming in California. But the fur farms failed due to the nutrias' destructive digging behavior and their need for huge amounts of food. Nutrias eat up to 25% of their body weight in vegetables every day. (Mink, in contrast, can thrive on small quantities of meat rendering by-products. Herbivores always require more food than carnivores.)

In the late 1930s unscrupulous promoters sold nutrias as aquatic weed cutters and for fur-raising "for fun and profit." Large numbers were imported to North America. It was hoped that they would be effective in clearing pond vegetation, but they went beyond this to eat useful plants as well. With the failure of the fur farms and the weed clearing projects, many of the animals were released into the wild, and others escaped from inadequate pens. They were hard to confine in pens because of their ability to dig out, and the concrete needed to contain them properly was too expensive.

Feral populations are now established in at least 15 states in the United States. Nutrias are highly gregarious, and wild nutrias are very tame. They don't seem to fear man.

Nutrias build burrows with several entrances, usually, and an underground nesting chamber. They build a variety of nests, from small, flattened areas of matted plant material to large platforms up to a meter high in shallow water. Nutrias like to dig their dens into a bank with a slope of 45 to 90 degrees. The insulation provided by the ground allows them to have a continuously mild temperature inside the den during winter.

Nutrias do not have a fixed season for breeding. Females dominate over males except when mating. Their young are fully furred and active at birth, ready to eat and swim. They are capable of surviving on their own, away from their mother, after only five days of nursing, but they generally nurse for six to ten weeks.

In Florida, nutrias are considered a nuisance. They maintain a wild breeding population in the state, unlike other escapees such as the domestic rabbit and ferret. They cause damage to drainage systems, crops, and natural plant communities. They feed on a broad range of crops, including corn, sugarcane, alfalfa, and rice. They pull up the seedlings of bald cypress trees and eat the roots. Their burrows penetrate mud banks up to 20 feet deep, causing damage to levees and commercial ponds. By eating all emerging vegetation they can completely clear the native plants from an area.

The major predator of nutrias in Florida is the alligator. Not only do alligators feed on nutrias in the wild, but nutrias are trapped and sold as food to the many alligator farms.

MK/DPA

△ Nutrias, like beavers, have lips that close behind their teeth so that they can harvest underwater vegetation without swallowing water. The mouth of the nutria in the photo above appears to be wide open, at first glance, but is actually tightly shut.

DOUBLE DIGESTION

Rabbits and certain other animals such as nutrias re-ingest their feces by eating them directly from the anus. The animals usually do this after returning to their nest at the end of their active period. There are two kinds of fecal pellets produced and only one kind is re-ingested. It is believed that re-ingestion is not merely an effort to derive more nutrition from the same food, but that certain essential vitamins are created in the digestive tract through this process.

SIDE NIPPLES

The female nutria has 4 or 5 pairs of nipples located on the side of her torso, a unique adaptation which allows her to suckle her young while swimming or to stand up to watch for predators while nursing young on the nest. No other North American mammal has mammary glands positioned in this manner.

THE NUTRIA FUR TRADE

The Nutria is the number one fur-bearing animal in Louisiana; there is a good demand for its belly fur. Most of the nutrias in Louisiana are descended from 20 individuals brought there in 1938. By the late 1950s there were an estimated 20 million nutrias in the state.

ANIMAL FUR

Hair, along with milk in mammary glands, is one of the key characteristics of mammals. All mammals have hair at some stage of their development (even if only a little bit such as the whales). No other vertebrates have hair. Some mammals have dense fur, while other mammals such as whales and elephants have only a few scattered bristles. The manatee has only a few hairs scattered over its body plus whiskers on its face.

Hair is composed primarily of the protein keratin, which is also found in fingernails, claws, hooves, and horns, and in the feathers of birds. Hair also contains the dark pigment melanin and other pigments.

Most mammals have three kinds of hair: facial whiskers which are sensitive to touch and which have sensing apparatus at the base of each hair; soft, fine hairs which make up the thick underfur of the animal; and longer guard hairs which protect this undercoat. The density of the hairs depends on the type of animal and the hairs' location on the animal. Sea otters have the thickest fur of any animal, with up to 1,000,000 hairs per square inch, and averaging perhaps 250,000 hairs per square inch. In contrast, humans (who are not balding) have only 100,000 hairs on their heads, far fewer than the sea otter has on a single square inch of its fur.

Hair has a number of different functions on mammals. Insulation is the obvious function; a thick coat of fur helps prevent heat loss in winter. Many animals, such as white-tailed deer, grow different winter and summer coats. The winter coats are many times heavier and provide better heat retention.

Hair provides buoyancy to some aquatic mammals. Sea otters trap air bubbles in their hair so they can float more easily— oil from spills prevents this. The otters also spread a water-repellent oil from their skin to their hair.

Polar bears have hollow, translucent hairs. These hairs allow sunlight to reach their dark skin, and this helps them absorb heat. In zoos, their fur may appear green, because algae sometimes grow on their hair.

Some animals regulate their body heat by fluffing out or flattening their fur. Fluffed up fur retains heat better, while flattened fur lets heat escape. Goosebumps on people may have served to fluff up our fur, long ago, when we had real fur.

Some animals have markings on their fur as babies which they lose as they grow up. Panther cubs and deer fawn are spotted, for example, but the adults are not. Young animals are more vulnerable to predators, and spots or other markings probably help protect the youngsters by providing camouflage.

The quills of porcupines are modified hairs. Not only are they sharp and stiff, but they have scales that point toward the base, unlike most hairs, so after the quills penetrate a victims flesh, they are hard to pull out. Another example of modified hair is the rhino's horn which is composed of compressed hairs.

EASTERN COTTONTAIL
(Sylvilagus floridanus)

The Eastern cottontail is the common American cottontail bunny, the most widely distributed rabbit in the United States. Most everyone is familiar with the classical literature referring to rabbits (Brer' Rabbit, the Tortoise and the Hare, Peter Rabbit). These childhood stories no doubt help create our

widely felt love affair with rabbits, cottontails in particular.

Almost everyone has seen a cottontail. The conspicuous, white, cotton-like tail is the source of its common name. When disturbed, it darts about on established trails in the grass or hops about the backyard or field. It feeds at night on plants and holes up during the day in thickets, although it sometimes feeds during the day as well.

A rabbit can take a bite out of a finger if one is put into its mouth, but generally rabbits are not dangerous. They rarely bite people, with the exception of tough old males or young males that are just coming of age.

Rabbits have a wide field of vision, and their eyes are far more light sensitive than those of man. Rabbits can dilate the blood vessels in their ears to radiate heat and thus keep cool. They can also use

▷ This cottontail is gathering grass to build a nest. Nests are made of plant material and lined with fur pulled from the mother's pelt.

◁ The underside of the tail is white, hence the name cottontail. The white tail functions like a flag which the babies can follow.

their big ears for shade or fold them down against the body as insulation against cold. Their ears are very tender. It is very painful for rabbits when people pick them up by the ears.

A rabbit's front teeth, the incisors, grow 3 to 4 inches per year. If rabbits eat the proper diet, their teeth wear down at the same rate as they grow.

The expression "breeds like a bunny" is a reflection of fact, since cottontails are very prolific, with up to 7 litters a year. However, the young rabbits are prey for nearly every predator of small mammals. Only one out of five cottontails survives to celebrate its first birthday, thereby keeping the population from exploding.

The female prepares a nest, a depression in the ground lined with grass and fur, where she gives birth to 3 to 7 naked, helpless young. At dusk and dawn she visits the nest and lies down over the opening, allowing the young to nurse. She feeds all night and rests apart from her young during the day.

People who find rabbits alone in their nests often assume they have been abandoned. Rabbits should be considered orphaned, however, only if the mother does not visit the nest within several hours after dark. At about two weeks of age the mother abandons her young completely, but by then they are already eating grass and no longer need her milk. Young rabbits are old enough to be on their own when they begin to voluntarily raise and lower their ears.

Cottontails are the most important small game mammal of the eastern United States. Their meat is a tasty delicacy for hunters, but their hide is of little value. Most farm kids start their hunting careers by shooting cottontails. Since rabbits can do severe damage to mom's garden and dad's crops, rural parents often allow their young children to get out the trusty .22, so they can proudly control the little pests just like dad and grandpa used to do.

Hunting cottontails is allowed year round in Florida, with a daily bag limit. However, they are not hunted as much in the South as in other regions. Rattlesnakes are a bit of a deterrent to hunters, and the threat of tularemia, or rabbit fever, is greater here than in the North. Tularemia is so highly contagious that gloves are recommended when cleaning rabbits, along with care to avoid cutting oneself. Cooking kills the organism.

▷ Baby bunnies in the nest, snuggling together for warmth.

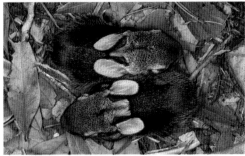

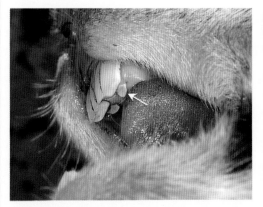

RABBIT TEETH

Rabbits have six incisors, the sharp front teeth usually used for cutting. They are arranged four above and two below. Two of the six are smaller and hidden behind the two more visible upper incisors. These two small, extra incisors clearly distinguish rabbits from rodents, which only have four incisors.

The two frontmost upper incisors of the rabbit are so deeply grooved that they give the appearance of four teeth. This is an anatomical feature without any known function. Some scientists speculate that in an earlier evolutionary period, the two grooved teeth might have actually been four teeth.

THE SPREAD OF RABBITS

During the early period of European exploration, rabbits were released on uninhabited islands in remote parts of the world in hopes they would provide a source of food for sailing vessels that might visit later. Rabbits were also introduced extensively in settled areas for the purpose of sport hunting. In third world countries in times past, rabbits were often the first thing missionaries and food organizations tried to introduce, because they reproduced so quickly. In this manner, the European rabbit was introduced around the world.

Releasing rabbits on these islands was a terrible mistake. In New Zealand and Australia, rabbits nearly destroyed the sheep raising industry because they ate the grasses. Rabbits became so common in Australia that rabbit meat was exported by the ton and eaten around the world. Rabbit fur is also of commercial value, although it is not very high in quality.

So far there has not been a rabbit problem in Florida, although the situation with the jackrabbits at Miami International Airport is something that needs to be monitored (see page 122).

MARSH RABBIT
(Sylvilagus palustris)

In comparison with a cottontail, a marsh rabbit is smaller, darker, and shorter-eared, with shorter hind legs and a smaller, darker tail. However, they are similar enough at first glance that many people have difficulty differentiating marsh rabbits from cottontails. Like cottontails, marsh rabbits are found throughout the Florida mainland, but marsh rabbits are the only rabbits in the lower Keys.

As their name indicates, marsh rabbits live in wetter areas, at the edges of salt marshes and mangrove swamps on barrier islands as well as inland lakes and marshes. They often create distinct tunnels through high grass around freshwater lake shores. Marsh rabbits usually walk instead of hopping in the manner of most rabbits. They swim routinely, unlike cottontails, and may actually hide or rest by floating in aquatic vegetation. To escape predation, they may swim out into a pond or stream with only their nose above water. It's not unusual to find a marsh rabbit swimming from island to island along Florida's coastline, hundreds of feet from land. This is despite the fact that marsh rabbits have no obvious adaptations for swimming.

△ Marsh rabbits can swim, in contrast to other rabbits which generally stay away from water. Their ability to swim helps them survive in their marshy habitat.

△ Note the very short legs and ears which help distinguish the marsh rabbit from the cottontail. The short legs may be an advantage in swampy areas, allowing this rabbit to scurry about on soft, wet ground. Hopping like other rabbits might cause it to sink into the muck.

STRANGE EATING HABITS

Rabbits and hares in the wild all eat a certain amount of excrement directly from their anus. This is re-digested immediately, so that much of their food goes through their digestive track twice. Feeding on stool is called "coprophagy." This practice completes the digestion of the plant matter and provides vitamins and protein which might not otherwise be found in the normal diet. This is something like a cow chewing its cud. The pellets which result from re-digested food look different from normal pellets. Domestic rabbits eat some of their feces as they are defecating, but many of the fecal pellets fall through the wire floors of their cages.

THE PLAYBOY BUNNY

Hugh Heffner, publisher of Playboy Magazine, funded research on a population of between 200 and 400 marsh rabbits found on a few islands in the lower Florida Keys. When these rabbits were found to be a unique subspecies, they were named after Mr. Heffner, Sylvilagus palustris hefneri. This is the only rabbit on the federal endangered list and one of six endangered mammal subspecies found only in the Florida Keys.

FLORIDA'S FOSSIL MAMMALS

The living mammals of Florida pale in comparison to the strange and wonderful beasts that inhabited the state in prehistoric times. Since the Florida peninsula first emerged above the ocean 25 million years ago, it has been home to an incredible variety of mammals. Many mammals that are thought to be typical of other continents were actually Florida natives as recently as 10,000 years ago.

Horses were reintroduced into North America by the Spanish about 500 years ago. However, during the last 25 million years, more than 50 species of one-toed and three-toed horses called Florida home prior to their extinction. Many species of llamas, as well as tapirs, peccaries, jaguars, and spectacled bears inhabited Florida, although today they are only found in South America. Rhinoceroses are now restricted to Africa and Asia, but several species of medium to large rhinos lived in Florida prior to their disappearance 5 million years ago. Elephants and their relatives are another group that was abundant and diverse in the Florida fossil record before they disappeared 10,000 years ago. Early Paleo-Indians in Florida coexisted with, and almost certainly hunted, the American mastodon and the Columbian mammoth.

The Florida landscape during earlier epochs was also inhabited by many strange mammals that were very different from the mammals of today. Examples include giant camels with long necks that stood nearly 15 feet tall, probably the New World's answer to the giraffe; giant elephant-like creatures called shovel-tuskers which had a pair of large, flattened tusks that protruded from the front of the lower jaw; and a bizarre distant relative of camels that had a y-shaped horn on its nose and two horns on the back of its skull that curved forward. These and other plant eaters were eaten by a large variety of carnivores. A sampling includes giant bear-dogs the size of Kodiak bears, another huge bear that was a relative of the greater panda from China, and a very large sabertooth.

About 2.5 million years ago an event called the Great American Interchange profoundly changed the character of Florida's mammals. At that time the Isthmus of Panama formed, joining the former island of South America with North America. Shortly after this connection, a weird assemblage of mammals previously restricted to South America invaded Florida. These immigrants included the glyptodont, a giant, thick-shelled relative of the armadillo that was similar in size and shape to a small car such as the Volkswagen beetle; another armadillo relative, the pampathere; plus the giant ground sloth which was nearly 20 feet tall when it stood on its hind legs. The Daytona Museum of Arts and Sciences has a spectacular mounted

△ Gary Morgan of the Florida Museum of Natural History holds the skull of a sabertooth and a leg bone of a mammoth. At left is the lower jawbone of a mastodon. All of these creatures have been found at sites within Florida.

skeleton of the giant ground sloth.

Paleo-Indians first entered Florida about 12,000 years ago. Within a few thousand years most of the large mammals had disappeared. Some scientists believe that human hunting was solely responsible for their extinction. Others believe it was a combination of this predation and changes in climate and vegetation.

△ Paleontology students heading for a dig at a Suwannee River fossil site. Some of the richest finds are in or near rivers such as the Aucilla, Ichetucknee, and Silver Rivers in North Florida. Many of the fossils from Florida's clear, spring-fed rivers are collected by amateur scuba divers.

△The pampathere (giant armadillo) closely resembled our living armadillo but was more than six feet long.

▷ A small boy shows the scale of a mastodon found at Wakulla Springs, now at the Florida Museum of Science and Natural History, Tallahassee.

Bobcat

BOBCAT
(*Felis rufus*)

Bobcats are very common in the wild in Florida. Their range extends throughout most of North America and Mexico, and they are found in a number of different habitats, including swamps, forests, deserts, mountains, and agricultural areas. In Florida, they often make their dens in dense palmetto thickets. They are also common in developed areas but seldom seen, in part because they are almost totally nocturnal.

Like domestic cats, bobcats purr, and they make screaming or squealing noises when in heat. These graceful cats are twice as big as domestic cats, however, and stronger. They have bobbed tails, and their ears have tufts of dark hair at the tips.

Bobcats are strictly carnivores but have a diverse diet. They help control the populations of rodents and rabbits, their most important prey, but they also eat reptiles, fish, birds, and insects. These agile, efficient predators also get into chicken coops and kill poultry, and they may even kill deer and hogs. They sometimes prey on domestic cats, so as they move into an area the population of domestic cats living in the wild may decrease.

Bobcats are solitary animals that usually come together only to breed. They live in shifting and sometimes overlapping territo-

△ Note the bobbed tail with a white tip which is characteristic of bobcats. Around the world there are a number of cats with bobbed tails. They are often grouped in a genus called *Lynx*. The cat in this photo also shows the characteristic pointed, black-tipped ear tufts.

ries (but usually not overlapping with the same sex), up to 10 square miles for the males, which they mark with scents—secretions from their anal glands as well as their feces and urine.

Bobcats sometimes interbreed with domestic cats, but this is probably very rare, and most of these interbreedings do not produce offspring. A bobcat is more likely to eat a housecat than mate with it. Most kittens with stubby tails are the offspring of domestic cats.

Bobcat kittens, averaging 2 to 3 in a litter, are reared solely by their mothers. Adult bobcats rarely fall prey to other animals, but the kittens may be eaten by foxes, coyotes, and owls, and they are sometimes killed by male bobcats. At about 6 months of age they disperse to find territories of their own.

Bobcats are extremely dangerous as pets because they often slash with razor-sharp claws. They are among the most dangerous of mammals to rehabilitate, and, unlike the Florida panther, it is almost impossible to tame them. They do not like to be cornered or confined; they often go crazy and badly injure themselves in live traps.

Bobcats are considered game in Florida, and they are valuable fur animals. Their very soft, dense fur is reddish brown, usually, with black or dark brown markings. The color and markings vary throughout their range, however, and Florida's bobcats are generally darker gray than those in other regions, with fewer markings. The pelts are used for hats, coats, and trim.

△ This bobcat demonstrates its hunting behavior.

▷ Like every other cat, bobcats have teeth which are modified for a strict meat-eating diet. They have fewer teeth, which increases the pressure exerted by each tooth, a shorter jaw for a more powerful bite, and all their teeth are sharp, including the molars! The enlarged canines are used to hold and stab the prey.

CUTE – BUT BEWARE!

Although cute and cuddly looking, even young bobcats are rarely tamed. They are ferocious animals and considered even more dangerous than a cheetah. The male bobcat sometimes kills the female when they mate, an example of how vicious they can become when excited. The cute little bobcat kitten at right was brought to a wildlife rehab center because its mother had been struck by a car. It attacked everyone within range, exhibiting a tremendous capacity to slash and bite. An adult bobcat can slash through a heavy leather workboot with one swipe.

△ Notice the blue eyes of this baby bobcat. Many baby cats, including panthers, have blue eyes. The blue eyes gradually change to brown as the cat matures.

◁ An exceptional baby bobcat which has been handled from birth by an experienced animal trainer. This docile pose is very unusual and deceptive.

BLACK BOBCATS

The Latin name of the bobcat, Felis rufus, means red cat. There have never been black panthers in Florida, not a single confirmed case, so it is thought that most reports of black panthers were probably sightings of black bobcats instead. Ten black or "melanistic" bobcats have been documented in southeastern Florida over the years; the latest, in 1990, weighed 25 to 30 pounds.

Melanism appears to be more common in moist, warm climates. It is unusual in big cats, except near the equator, but it is relatively common among gray and fox squirrels, red foxes, and minks. An abundance of the dark pigment "melanin" causes the black color, but brown and other colors may be present, too. In the case of melanistic bobcats, the normal markings can be seen through the black when the animal is in bright light.

Panther

FLORIDA PANTHER
(Felis concolor coryi)

The Florida panther is a subspecies of the cougar, a large cat that once roamed from the Yukon to the tip of South America but now is extinct through much of its former range. The panther has many common names including mountain lion, cougar, puma, and catamount.

Today, the Florida panther is the only large cat living in the wild east of the Mississippi. In the American West and in South America, cougars still exist, but the Florida panther, a subspecies, is on the brink of extinction. With an estimated 30 to 50 individuals left, the panther is considered by many experts to be one of the most endangered mammals in the world.

The remaining Florida panthers now live in the Big Cypress National Preserve (plus adjacent private lands), and Everglades National Park, both in the southern part of the state.

All research on the Florida panther has centered on this South Florida population, and the Florida Game Commission does not officially acknowledge that any panthers exist elsewhere. Although there have been sightings by knowledgeable observers scattered around the state, and the panther is an elusive animal, most experts believe there are no panthers living undetected in other parts of the Florida.

Florida panthers were hunted relentlessly in earlier years by ranchers who wished to protect their cattle, while deer hunters reduced the number of deer which were their main food source. Lately, the biggest threat has been the rapid destruction of their habitat due to development.

Panthers need a lot of space for hunting and breeding. Overdevelopment and the southward expansion of the citrus industry has resulted in the loss of many areas formerly suitable for panthers, and what were once extensive forests have become isolated fragments. With the remaining population so small, inbreeding has become a big problem.

▽ A typical lair (resting place or den) of a panther. Florida panthers don't dig their dens. They usually find a crevice under roots, fallen trees, or palmettos. This particular photo was taken near a stream bed.

The cougar has been considered a serious pest species in the west, because the big cats killed sheep and cattle. But in Florida, although panthers may have occasionally killed livestock, they were never a major pest. They preferred deer and wild hogs. However, they were perceived as a threat, and the loss of panthers was due in part to hunting as well as loss of habitat.

For years, hunting of cougars was encouraged nationwide by a bounty system. In Florida, a $5.00 bounty was paid for panther pelts until late in the last century. Sport hunting of cougars is still allowed in most western states. California has banned sport hunting, and many states are likely to follow because cougar populations are decreasing.

The Florida panther was first protected by Florida law in 1958 and listed as an endangered subspecies by the United States in 1967. It was further protected by the Florida Panther Act of 1978. Recovery programs to save the panther began in 1976 and were thoroughly revised in 1987.

The Florida panther became the official animal of the state of Florida in 1982, after it was overwhelmingly chosen by elementary school children over the alligator and manatee. Most legislators originally favored the alligator, but the children prevailed. (The alligator is now the official state reptile, and the manatee is now the official state marine mammal, so for once, everyone won!)

△ Panthers need a vast area in which to hunt. Males range over 200 square miles, and a large male will range over as much as 500 square miles. Panthers usually walk 15 to 20 miles a day in a zigzag pattern, often moving through a narrow corridor from one hunting area to another. They travel day and night in winter, but mostly at night in summer. They swim readily and sometimes cross wide bodies of water.

◁ Panthers are not extremely vocal, but they do have a repertory of sounds which includes screams on occasion. They use their retractable claws to climb trees and for catching prey. Their tracks somewhat resemble those of large dogs, but without the claws showing (although the presence or absence of claw marks is not as significant as the overall shape of the print).

Panther

Panthers mate in January or February, at which time males and females may travel together briefly. Baby panthers are born in a den, which in Florida is just a small pocket or niche, often in a thicket of palmettos. The kittens' eyes are blue when they first open, about a week after birth, but their color changes to a yellowish brown as the kittens mature.

The kittens usually remain with their mother for 12 to 18 months. They are helpless for the first 2 months. The mother goes out from the den periodically to hunt for food, leaving the kittens alone for up to 36 hours.

The kittens learn to hunt through play. When the mother is

▷ The cougar is born spotted, and with rings on its tail, but the spots fade as the kitten ages, and after about a year it will have lost all of its spots. Florida panthers are tawny and dark-colored, often reddish-brown, with lighter, gray underparts. There are no black cougars or black Florida panthers—they do not exist. People who report seeing a black panther may have seen a large, black bobcat, or some other animal such as an otter or even a dark (but not black) panther which might seem black in dim light.

ready to wean them, she makes a kill, and while the young are busy feeding she will leave the area. The young ones soon disperse and seek their own territories. They may survive for about 12 years in the wild.

△ The supremely majestic look of the adult panther is due in part to the unique shape of its skull, which gives the profile a long, smooth line from the top of the head to the tip of the nose.

△ Wild animals are often selected as pets because they are cute and cuddly as infants. Later, however, this baby will become 120 pounds of dangerous and unmanageable cat.

62

Panther's are found in a wide range of forested habitats including hardwood hammocks, pine flatwoods, and swamp forests, far from people. These forests are home to the panthers' favorite prey, the white-tailed deer.

A single panther may consume from 35 to 50 deer a year (or ten times that number of raccoons). Wild hogs are also a major food of Florida panthers, and they eat armadillos, birds, raccoons, and rabbits as well.

Panthers stalk their prey and then jump and break its neck with a single bite through the spinal cord. They eat what they can, cover their kill with dirt and leaves, and come back the next day. They usually eat the intestinal tract of their prey first. A panther tends to remain in the area of its kill, eating more as it gets hungry, until the kill is entirely consumed or becomes too rotten to eat.

Panthers can run very fast, up to 35 miles an hour, but only for a few hundred yards, so they have to make the kill quickly. Their prey usually have greater endurance and can run for hours.

Panthers are solitary animals. They mark their territories by using their hind feet to make "scrapes," little piles of leaves and material on which they defecate and urinate. They make these piles using an alternate treading motion with their hind feet. Even captive panthers like to make scrapes. The making of scrapes is not unique to panthers, however. Bobcats do the same thing.

PANTHERS AS PETS

There are over 700 captive cougars in Florida kept legally as pets through state-issued permits. Although cute and cuddly when small, they soon become powerful animals which are difficult to manage, and most become unwanted.

The cougars kept as pets in Florida are not true Florida panthers. A full-blooded Florida panther would be immediately confiscated by the Florida Game Commission and placed in a state facility. Western cougars are inexpensive, costing only a few hundred dollars, but they do not make good pets when fully grown. Even though they may become quite tame, their strength is

overwhelming. Also, there is always the chance that a captive animal will be released or escape.

In captivity, baby cougars are very difficult to keep alive and raise on a bottle. Their mortality rate is about 50 percent.

Since 1981, Florida's panthers have been studied using collars with radio transmitters. Panthers are tracked and treed by specially trained hounds, anesthetized with tranquilizer from a dart gun, and lowered with a rope and harness, or caught with a net or blanket as they fall from the tree. Captured panthers are given a thorough examination, radio collared, and then released. Often they are inoculated against diseases as well.

Nearly all the known panthers in the Florida wilds have been caught and collared in this manner. They are tracked several times a week, and their locations are plotted on maps. In this manner, much has been learned about their behavior.

In a 10 year period, 1978 to 1988, 11 of 20 known Florida Panther deaths were caused by cars, primarily on Alligator Alley and State Route 29. Five panthers were also shot in that same period. (Seminole-Miccosukee Indians feel that the use of panthers is a necessary part of their rituals and have come into conflict with the legal system over this issue, although they are not responsible for all the shooting deaths.)

Now I-75 has been fenced to protect animals from cars, with tunnels every few miles so animals can cross under the road. Surveillance videos of these newly constructed underground tunnels show that they are used regularly by panthers and other animals.

PHYSICAL CHARACTERISTICS

The Florida panther has been characterized by a crook in its tail, a whorl or cowlick of hair in the middle of its back, and white flecks on its neck. However, the crook and the cowlick have been linked to inbreeding rather than characters that identify a distinct subspecies, and most, but not all, cougars in Florida have these traits. The white flecks are probably caused by skin irritations resulting from tick bites, as ticks are extremely abundant in the areas inhabited by panthers. The main physical characteristic which actually distinguishes the Florida panther from other subspecies of cougar is the shape of the skull. Also, the body hair of the Florida panther is relatively short and its legs relatively long compared to other populations.

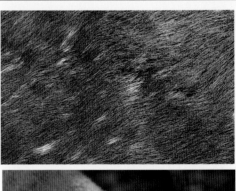

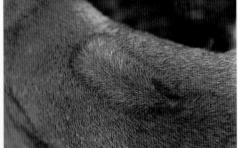

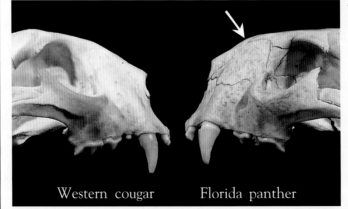

Western cougar   Florida panther

◁ This photo shows the skulls of the western cougar and the Florida panther. The arrow indicates the exaggerated rise of the nasal arch, one of the main characteristics which distinguishes the Florida panther from its western relatives.

PLACEMENT OF EYES

Plant-eating animals such as deer usually have good vision over 270 degrees, every direction except directly behind. Their eyes are positioned on the sides of their heads so they can watch in all directions for predators. These animals don't have good binocular vision, which is necessary for depth perception. Animals which hunt prey for food usually have their eyes on the front of their heads. Panthers have a field of vision of only about 130 degrees. They lack the panoramic view of the herbivores, but they have excellent depth perception for capturing prey.

Nocturnal hunters must be able to locate prey in very dim light. These animals, including cats, have pupils which are capable of opening very wide. In addition, they have a special reflecting layer which reflects light that has entered the eye back to the retina so that it has a second chance of stimulating a receptor. This is why when a bright light hits a nocturnal animal there is so much eye shine. Cats can see in light only 1/6 as bright as humans require.

THE CAPTIVE BREEDING PROGRAM

Humans were largely responsible for the decline of the Florida panther, but without human intervention now, their extinction is almost certain. Ideas for protecting the Florida panther range from doing absolutely nothing to removing people and vehicles from panther areas, eliminating all disturbances, and restricting development of lands where Florida panthers are found, to capturing all the remaining Florida panthers and putting them into captive breeding programs before they become extinct.

A captive breeding program was started in 1991 in an effort to enhance the Florida panthers' genetic variability. One goal of panther conservationists is to reintroduce Florida panthers to suitable areas where they were formerly found, such as the Osceola National Forest.

However, the trial introduction program used western cougars, not Florida panthers. Since western cougars are the same species as the Florida panther, fertility, breeding, and reintroduction have been studied using captive western cougars to avoid jeopardizing the few remaining Florida panthers.

Florida panthers have many health problems. Feline distemper is a problem, and hookworms and other parasites often result in anemia. Due to inbreeding, over 90% of the sperm of Florida male panthers is abnormal. Many males have only one testicle, but they are still able to breed and have offspring. Many panthers captured in the wild were also found to have heart murmurs recently.

Until recently, the most popular solution for the declining panther population problem

△ This panther is wearing a mask for anesthesia.

was the captive breeding program, which began with the capture from the wild of animals deemed to have the purest Florida panther characteristics (identified through genetic testing). Techniques such as forced ovulation, artificial insemination, and the distribution of the fertilized eggs to surrogate mothers (using non-endangered cougars from the west) were employed. It was hoped that a large enough captive population could be developed in this manner to allow offspring to be released into the wild. Unfortunately, the outcome of releasing captive-bred cougars in the wild is uncertain. Many things must be considered. Does enough space exist for a population of breeding size to survive? Is there sufficient prey? Will local communities accept the presence of a large and powerful cat?

◁ This photo commemorates the first surgically assisted fertilization of a Florida panther. One of the several procedures performed that day was successful.

Panther

PHOTO MODELS

Several Floridians own panthers and rent them to nature photographers. These entrepreneurs are in a strange "catch-22" situation. They must assure the photographers that their animals are genuine Florida panthers. However, it is illegal to possess a true Florida panther, so they must claim to Fish and Game officers that their animals are only partly Florida panther and mostly western cougar. Oddly enough, both the photographers and the game officers seem to be satisfied with the explanations. A number of the photos in this book show animals which are not pure Florida panthers, although the differences would be hard to detect. The purest remaining specimens are carefully protected and are not generally available for photography.

PANTHER PUBLICATIONS

The Coryi is a newsletter about the panther published by the Florida Game and Freshwater Fish Commission, 620 South Meridian St., Tallahassee, FL 32399-1600. Subscription is free (financed by tax deductible contributions to the Florida Panther Research and Management Trust Fund) and brings another publication, The Skimmer.

POLITICS OF THE PANTHER

The Florida panther's tale is a sad story. Thirty million dollars have been spent by a number of federal and state agencies, and yet the Florida panther is as close to extinction today as when the efforts to save it began (although much scientifically valuable information has been learned along the way).

There has been a lot of disagreement among experts about what is the best way to protect and preserve this magnificent creature. This controversy combined with the large amounts of government money involved in the program has spawned much publicity and many legal actions. Throughout it all the Florida public has remained very supportive of the efforts to help the panther. Here are some of the most interesting highlights of the panther story.

The Trial of James Billy: At his trial for killing a panther, Seminole Chief James Billy argued in his defense that the average person cannot tell the difference between a protected native Florida panther and a western cougar which is an introduced, non-native cat, and thus not legally protected. Billy was not convicted, although the court did not specifically rule on this argument.

Even at the time that James Billy killed the panther, there was a provision (sometimes called the "look-alike law") in the federal Endangered Species Act which prohibits the killing of animals that are similar in appearance to endangered animals. However, at the time of the killing, official action had not been taken to activate the look-alike provision for the Florida panther. In response to the Billy trial and other similar cases, this action has since been taken. Also, the state of Florida now has a similar law.

The Fund For Animals Lawsuit: At one time, the most popular plan for saving the panther population in Florida was the captive breeding program (see details on page 65). Fund for Animals, an animal rights group, took legal action to stop the capture of wild panthers for the captive breeding program because they wanted to force a confrontation with the state about destruction of habitat, which they believed to be the primary problem. Fund for Animals argued that efforts to save the panther should be focused on the preservation and restoration of suitable habitat, and that without this, all other efforts were bound to fail. While not opposed to captive breeding, they did oppose the removal of adult animals from the wild population. They argued that this could disrupt the social organization of the remaining panthers and proposed that only kittens be taken. A compromise settlement was eventually reached and the program proceeded.

The Need for Outbreeding: The captive breeding program was based on the idea that the purest specimens should be selected from the wild in order to preserve as much as possible the unique characteristics of the Florida panther. However, because of the small number of remaining animals, inbreeding has already occurred. This inbreeding may be the cause of congenital heart defects and other problems which are now found in some Florida panthers. The latest thinking is that in order to save the Florida population of panthers, it may be necessary to bring in a limited number of western cougars to breed with them.

The Importance of the Endangered Subspecies Designation: One definition of a subspecies is a geographic population which shares certain subtle physical characteristics that distinguishes it from other geographic populations of the same species. At one time cougars inhabited the southeastern states and intermingled with cougars from other regions of the country. Because of loss of habitat due to human settlements, cougars became extinct in all the states east of the Mississippi River except Florida. The small population remaining in Florida survived, but has been isolated for at least 150 years.

Western cougars are relatively abundant and are not protected in the western states, whereas the small remaining population of big cats in Florida (a subspecies) is extremely endangered and thus given strong protection.

Critics of the various programs to save the panther have suggested that the remaining Florida panthers may no longer be a unique subspecies because of dilution from possible breeding with non-native cougars. Some cougars of mixed heritage were released into the Everglades in the 1950s by the Park Service in an attempt to enhance that population. However, genetic studies and comparison with museum specimens have convinced most scientists that the dilution has been minimal.

Is Saving the Florida Panther Worth the Effort? The public's keen interest in the fate of the Florida panther has certainly helped build awareness of other conservation programs. Large cats are interesting and help focus public attention on conservation. Preservation of genetic diversity is always desirable. The fact that the Florida panther has survived this long in spite of all the hazards may indicate that it has developed certain special adaptations to the Florida environments. Florida environments differ greatly from the dryer environments of Texas and the colder climates of the North. If this is the case, attempts to reintroduce western cougars to Florida should the Florida panther become extinct might not succeed because these animals may not be adapted physiologically or behaviorally to the heat and humidity of Florida.

Perhaps most importantly, conserving a large predator with large land requirements helps conserve all the other species which depend on that same environment. New species arise and others become extinct as part of natural processes, but the imminent extinction of the panther is something that has been caused by human activity and would not have occurred otherwise. A species can be a barometer for the condition of the environment. If panthers cannot survive in Florida, what species will be the next to go?

Many people believe that Florida panthers are so unique and such an important part of natural Florida, that it is worth every effort to save them and re-establish a viable breeding population. This may be especially true because the loss of the Florida panther could have a strong negative effect on other conservation efforts.

The story of the bureaucratic tangles involved in the efforts to save the panther is told in a newly released book, **Twilight of the Panther**, by Ken Alvarez. The book is available for $19.95 plus shipping and tax from BookWorld, 1933 Whitfield Loop, Suite 300, Sarasota, FL 34243.

Foxes

GRAY FOX
(Urocyon cinereoargenteus)

Gray foxes are widespread throughout the United States and are the smallest wild canines in Florida. Gray foxes are found throughout Florida, except in the Keys. They make their dens in wood piles, fallen trees, culverts, gopher tortoise burrows, and under mobile homes. Gray foxes are sometimes seen in trees. Their nails enable them to climb trees easily, although they do not climb like bears or cats, but rather by shimmying up the trunk and leaping from limb to limb.

The gray fox has coarse, silver-gray fur on its back with reddish sides and underside and a blackish tail tip. Its tail is one way to distinguish it from the red fox, whose tail has a distinctive white tip, and whose overall color is much redder. Fortunately for the gray fox, its fur is not valuable, and it is not as popular for hunting as the red fox because it will not give the hounds as good a chase.

Not quite as speedy as the red fox, this small, graceful animal is still capable of reaching 35 mph in short bursts. Its wide-ranging diet includes small mammals, birds, reptiles, insects, and plants. Both species of fox eat fruit, including grapes and persimmons in Florida, like the fox in Aesop's famous fable.

Foxes are seldom seen, in part because they are usually out only at night (although they are sometimes active during the day).

△ Gray foxes are most commonly seen in woodlands or at the edges of stands of trees. Red foxes are more common in open fields.

WHY MOST FEMALE MAMMALS BLEED AT THE PEAK OF THEIR FERTILITY CYCLES

In humans and other primates, the time of bleeding at the end of the menstrual cycle is the time when pregnancy is least likely. Yet most people are familiar with the fact that when their dogs or cats come into heat, their moment of maximum fertility, these females experience considerable vaginal bleeding. However, the bleeding that occurs when these female mammals are "in heat" is not menstrual bleeding. This bleeding is caused by the high level of sex hormones which peaks during heat.

Dogs, cats, and most other mammals also undergo a menstrual cycle similar to humans. The bleeding which occurs during this cycle is minimal, however, and usually goes unnoticed, thus giving the false impression that the blood observed during "heat" is the result of the menstrual cycle.

Both species are shy and elusive, but the gray fox is more common in Florida than the red fox. It is also more comfortable around human habitation, where it may feed on garbage, or come into yards to eat cat food. Where the red fox and the gray fox occupy the same area, the smaller gray fox is dominant, capable of pushing the red fox out of its territory if it chooses.

Gray foxes most often die not from natural causes but causes associated with man, including dog packs, guns, traps, automobiles, and pet diseases.

△ This gray fox mother is nursing her young offspring. They may venture out of the den to play at about three to four weeks, but only under the watchful eye of the mother. They do not leave home until about six months.

The gray fox is very susceptible to rabies and canine distemper. The overt symptoms of these two neurological diseases are identical. Dogs can get these diseases from contact with foxes if not protected by vaccination. Humans should avoid direct contact with a sick or strangely behaving fox because of the danger of rabies.

△ Gray foxes are charcoal color at birth.

◁ Gray foxes use tree limbs as resting places. Red foxes do not climb trees.

RED FOX (*Vulpes vulpes*)

The red fox has bright, red-orange fur, a black nose and paws, and a white-tipped tail. It weighs only five to fifteen pounds.

It was formerly found in Florida only in the northern part of the state, but its range has expanded southward and it is now found throughout the entire peninsula. It is widespread throughout the northern hemisphere, in part because it was widely introduced by fox hunters and in part because it is a very adaptable creature. Silver fox and cross fox are names sometimes given different color phases of the red fox.

The reputation of this fox as a sly, cunning animal is well deserved. A red fox will sometimes feign sleep to catch a rabbit. It more often hunts like a cat, however, slinking to get close to its prey and then running and pouncing on it. It is an unusually swift animal. It can run especially fast in short bursts, making it capable of occasionally catching a small deer.

Like the gray fox, the red fox is an opportunistic omnivore, eating whatever is available, including fruits. Rodents, rabbits, and birds are its preferred foods.

During the mating season, in winter and early spring, the males exude a musky odor from scent glands near the base of their tails, and they bark more at night. After they mate, both parents work together to raise their young, staying together until the pups leave home. Both red and gray foxes may use the same dens year after year.

BABY RED FOXES

Red foxes rear their young in underground dens. They may dig their own dens or modify the burrows of other animals.

The pups are helpless at birth, and their mother will remain with them for several days before leaving the den. At about one month, the pups begin romping and playing above ground, and they are taught how to hunt. They are nursed for about 2 months and leave home when they are about 6 months old.

◁ This is a baby "silver fox," a color variety of the red fox, which is mostly black at this stage. As it matures, it will have longer "guard hairs," with white tips which will give it a silvery appearance.

△ Although the gray fox has some prominent reddish color, it never has the bright red-orange color or the white-tipped tail which distinguishes the red fox.

△ This red fox is guarding a cache of food by displaying a defensive posture.

Like the gray fox, the red fox is susceptible to rabies and canine distemper. It also carries canine heartworm and is capable of passing this disease to a dog via mosquitoes, unless the pet is protected with heartworm preventative. However, as with the gray fox, the primary causes of death of red foxes are associated with man.

One of the saddest communicable diseases of the red fox is Sarcoptes mange, commonly called scabies. An intense scratching reaction to the mite which is associated with this disease causes the fox's eyes to swell. Whole populations of juvenile and adult foxes have been decimated by scabies. Pet dogs and people are also susceptible, but both are easily treated.

FOX HUNTS

The red fox is well-known as a "sporting" animal whose hunting is regulated. It is the fox commonly hunted in fox hunts (in some "hunts" the fox is chased but not killed), and it is also valued for its pelt. However, northern foxes have thicker and longer fur than Florida foxes, so their pelts are more in demand.

A TRUE FLORIDA NATIVE?

Red foxes were imported to the United States and released by hunting clubs for well over 100 years, until the middle of this century. It was once thought that the species was not native here, and that all red foxes now found in the United States are descendants of these imported animals.

Most mammalogists now believe that red foxes lived in the eastern United States long before the arrival of the European colonists, but that their numbers were small and they were not widespread until relatively recently. The native red foxes, it is thought, were invigorated by interbreeding with the European introductions (members of the same species), resulting in a great increase in their numbers and range. The correct interpretation of what happened is still subject to dispute, however.

RED WOLF
(*Canis rufus*)

Red wolves resemble small German shepherds. The name "red" is misleading. Although the coat is tinged with red, the background hair color is gray or black. There is also a black color phase.

Red wolves were found primarily in forests in Florida but also in prairies and coastal marshes. Their behavior is similar to that of the coyote, a smaller species of wild dog whose appearance is very similar to that of the 40 to 80 pound wolves. Male-female pairs mate for life, or until one dies, establishing territories and rearing their pups together. They use natural or excavated dens for shelter and rearing their young.

Red wolves prey primarily on small mammals, such as rabbits, rodents, and raccoons. Our perception of them as vicious predators that might attack people or livestock was highly unjust. The red wolf has never been known to attack people, and attacks on livestock were uncommon.

These wolves' story is a sad one, because they were almost completely exterminated in the wild through hunting and trapping and also the clearing of land for agriculture. The last ones were removed for captive breeding.

The bad reputation of the red wolf was based on the habits of the gray wolf and made worse by superstition and misunderstanding. The gray wolf is indeed a large, powerful, very aggressive animal. European folk tales featured fear of wolves, from stories about werewolves to the story about the wolf harassing the three little pigs, and even the story of Little Red Riding Hood. Many attacks by wolves were recorded in Europe, and during hard winters gray wolves sometimes terrorized entire villages.

Red wolves once ranged from the Mississippi Valley to Illinois and throughout the Southeast all the way to the tip of Florida, intermingling only slightly in the

northernmost portion of their range with the gray wolf, which is found in parts of northern and western United States. However, persecution of the red wolf reduced its range to the Gulf Coast of Texas and Louisiana by the early 1970s, nearly causing its extinction.

It seems that it is part of human nature to become emotional and fearful about animals that are not understood but are seen as threatening; a common reaction is to want to destroy such creatures. The word "wolf" rates right up there with "grizzly" and "rattlesnake" in bringing out this trait of mankind. Only recently has there been more understanding and appreciation of wolves.

In the 1880s there was a $5 bounty on red wolves in Florida; the bounty also included panthers and bears. The last known pure wolf in Florida was killed in 1908, and the last hybrid in 1917. In other parts of the Southeast, where they once numbered in the thousands, they disappeared from the wild in the 1970s.

A POSSIBLE PROBLEM WITH THIS SPECIES

There is now a scientific controversy about whether the red wolf is really a valid, distinct species, and there is some chance that in the future scientists may reclassify it. Recent genetic studies have indicated that the red wolf may actually be a cross between the gray wolf and the coyote, with some domestic dog genes thrown in for good measure. The researchers sampled DNA taken from red wolf skins in the Smithsonian Museum which were over 100 years old and even they contained unmistakable coyote genes. Further, there is no fossil evidence of the red wolf existing in Florida in earlier eras. The single fossil record of a red wolf from Florida is only a few hundred years old.

◁ Nine-week old pups in a den dug five feet into sand. The pups must stay in the den during daylight to remain safe from large predators such as bobcats and panthers. At the age of a few weeks, they start venturing out at night when their parents are present.

A SUCCESSFUL PROGRAM

The captive breeding and reintroduction program to save the red wolf has proven that nearly extinct animal species can be bred back to significant population levels, at least in captivity. It has been so successful that wildlife officials hoping to save other species now point to it as an example of what can be done.

In 1970, 17 red wolves, the last ones known, were trapped and shipped to Tacoma, Washington, where a captive breeding program was started. In 1980 the species was categorized as extinct in the wild. Since the captive breeding program started, the number of red wolves has risen to over 200, but the red wolf is still one of the rarest mammal species in the United States. Little is known about the species because so few have been available in recent decades for study.

The U.S. Fish and Wildlife Service, which oversees the Tacoma program, also started breeding programs on several barrier islands, including St. Vincent Island National Wildlife Refuge off the Florida Panhandle. Barrier islands were chosen because their isolation makes it easier to control the wolves and study the results of the program.

On the mainland, red wolves have been released in the Great Smoky Mountains National Park and at the Alligator River National Wildlife Refuge in North Carolina. Since their release, adult wolves with pups have been seen in North Carolina, which is an encouraging development. It is still not known whether these efforts will succeed, however. Competition and interbreeding with the increasingly numerous

This map show the locations of the zoos and wildlife centers which are participating in this program.

coyotes may be a problem. Nevertheless, the sheer determination and diligence of Roland Smith (the head of the U.S. Fish and Wildlife Service who started the red wolf breeding program in Tacoma) and others has at least temporarily saved the red wolf from extinction.

In Florida, there are only about 10 red wolves today, and they can be seen only in zoos or on St. Vincent Island. The Tallahassee Junior Museum and the Lowry Park Zoo in Tampa are among the zoological parks participating in the captive breeding program for red wolves.

Coyote

COYOTE
(Canis latrans)

The coyote is one of the most adaptable native mammals in North America. Its Latin name means "barking dog," and the coyote does resemble a dog. It looks like a small, short-legged, gray-colored German shepherd, or a small wolf. The coyote's color is a blend of gray with some red.

Coyotes are common in Native American art and folklore, and extraordinary abilities were often attributed to them. The name coyote (pronounced ki-o'-ti) comes from the Aztec word for them, *coyotl*.

A century ago the coyote was a western desert mammal, but today it can be found from the middle of Alaska to Central America and throughout eastern North America. It has adapted to nearly all types of habitats from deserts to swamps. It may have been driven to expand its range when its original homeland was disturbed by ranching and large-scale agriculture. It may also have been responding to the availability of more open land in the East, and the loss of the next larger species, the wolf, may have created a niche for the coyote in some areas.

The coyote was not seen east of the Mississippi until the 1950s, but it is now established in northern Florida and is increasingly reported farther south. It was probably introduced to the eastern United States when hunting clubs that had ordered red foxes accidentally received and released some coyotes, which are very similar to foxes when young. The coyote also probably moved east, at least in part due to a natural expansion of its range. Although there have been releases in several locations in Florida, coyotes are most common now in the northern part of the state. They are also common in parts of Georgia and Alabama and eastern United States.

Coyotes have an acute sense of hearing. They can hear a mouse squeak several hundred yards away. Their sight and smell are also excellent but their sense of taste is poorly developed. Noted for their baying, often in

duets, coyotes vocalize most frequently at dusk and dawn. The "song" of one coyote may be answered by another miles away.

Coyotes generally eat only small mammals and birds and it is unusual for them to prey on livestock. They are opportunistic feeders, taking their food alive or dead. They eat many rabbits and rodents. Any large mammal parts found in their stomach are usually from carrion.

A female coyote in a breeding condition will attract many males, and it is thought that she may select her mate from among the competitors. The male and

COYDOGS

Coyotes have interbred with gray wolves, red wolves, and domestic dogs, resulting in fertile offspring. However, the coyote-dog crosses, called "coydogs," are not successful hybrids and never survive longer than a few generations. A female coyote or coydog depends on the father to help feed and defend her young. Since pure dog fathers don't do this—they "skip town" instead—only a small percentage of coydog infants survive.

COYOTE PROBLEMS IN FLORIDA?

Because the coyote is a relative newcomer to this state and found here only in limited numbers, Florida has hardly any livestock predation by coyotes. There is also little evidence that they kill deer. Nevertheless, they are considered pests in Florida and receive no protection. It will be interesting to see if the coyote population blossoms here as it has in other states. Although coyotes have the potential to become a problem for ranchers in Florida, their potential effect on native wildlife is a more serious concern. Their competition might, for example, pose a threat to native foxes and the bobcat.

When sheep arrived in the West, coyotes discovered a delectable source of food. Immediately, the coyotes provoked an enor- *mous hatred, especially among herders, which persists to this day. Thus, the coyote has received one of the most profoundly negative responses of all of America's mammals. However, in part for this reason, the coyote has been very intensely studied.*

The United States government spent about $8 million for coyote control in 1971 alone. Man has placed a bounty on, shot, trapped, implanted with hormones, poisoned, and fenced coyotes, but the population still increases. Efforts to control the coyote have failed due to lack of information about this mammal. This western barking dog, this symbol of hatred and fear, has spread to all types of terrain throughout all contiguous forty-eight states, having overcome all the obstacles man has yet to devise.

female may mate year after year and use the same underground den for many years, but not necessarily for life. The den, a hole in the ground, may be the abandoned den of another animal.

The female usually gives birth in spring when small game is plentiful. When the pups are two weeks old, both parents begin to feed them regurgitated food, and after a short while the male can raise the pups successfully even if the female should die. The male and the previous year's offspring often hunt as a unit to feed the female and newborns.

The coyotes' family togetherness and their intelligence have undoubtedly helped make them successful survivors. Coyotes seem to prosper in the company of man, often living in the suburbs of western cities. They usually run in small groups of two adults, several young adult offspring, and pups if it is springtime.

Although the coyote's only natural predator was the wolf and its primary enemy today is man, distemper, rabies, mange, heartworm, and other parasites are also causes of coyote deaths.

ANIMAL SIGNS

Wild animals are shy and elusive creatures. Many are active only at night, live underground, or live in dense vegetation. Even those animals that live near humans, such as raccoons and opossums, prefer to remain undetected. Of all the species of Florida mammals, how many are commonly seen? The gray squirrel is active during daylight and is conspicuous. Fox squirrels are not uncommon although they have restricted habitats. Occasionally, it is possible to glimpse a deer or a rabbit by the side of the road, or the eye-shine of a fox or... something.. while driving down a narrow road at night. But most wild animals are rarely encountered.

However, mammals and other animals leave signs of their presence which are more likely to be seen than the animals themselves. The most common signs of animals are their tracks, but other clues to their presence include runways, burrows, nests, mounds, scrapes, and scat (feces).

Tracks*: Tracks left in sand or in mud along a creek are sometimes very clear, and most mammals, at least the medium to large mammals, are identifiable by their tracks. Tracks indicate how large the animal is, how many toes are present, the size of the front foot versus the back foot, features that when considered together reveal the identity of the animal.*

Felines (cats) and canines (dogs, foxes, wolves) can be of the same size and have similar footprints. Both walk on the balls of their feet, so both have a very short track, and there is no impression of a heel. The main difference is that cats have retractable claws (which helps keep their claws sharp) and dogs do not. A dog print will often show the impression of a claw, while the footprint of a cat would not. By comparison, bears and raccoons walk flat on their feet like humans, so their tracks show a heel impression for the hind foot.

Deer, cows, goats, pigs, and horses walk on their toes (or hooves). As with the felines and canines mentioned above, this lifting of the heel is an adaptation for running which effectively lengthens the leg. Deer have two toes on each foot and their tracks are different than those of horses which have only a single toe. There is something a little different about each track that can help make an identification (provided it is a good track), but it is not always easy. Tracks are often not clear. A track in

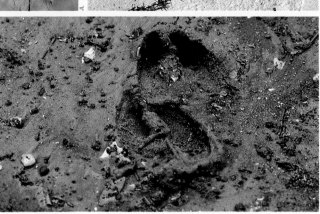

Above: The nest of a golden mouse.
Above right: The burrow of a beach mouse.
Right: The tracks of a white-tailed deer.

sand looks different than a track in mud. It takes time to become skilled in tracking.

Scat*: Scats (feces) from different animals vary in shape, size, and content, and also in the manner of deposition. For example, cats mark their territory with feces, urine, and scent, and often attempt to cover it by scraping soil and leaves with their back feet, leaving a rectangular swath called a "scrape." Otters deposit their feces in communal latrines or on high ground as a means of advertising their presence. These deposits may also be accompanied by scrapes. Biologists often collect the scat of the animals they study to analyze the contents and learn what the animals have been eating. This provides valuable information about the community of animals present in a specific habitat as well as the nutritional needs of the larger animals. Seeds, hair, bone fish, scales, shells and insect hard parts come through the digestive track relatively unchanged and can often be identified to the species level.*

Owl pellets are the dried, regurgitated bone and hair balls which represent the indigestible parts of an animal eaten by an owl. They are found in a heap beneath the tree where an owl has been feeding. Although they are not produced by a mammal, they can reveal much about the small mammals present. Over time, owl food can track changes in the community of animals. For example, it can signal the introduction of an exotic species or an invasion of Norway or black rats. When the pellets are pulled apart, they reveal skulls, limb bones, and hair, all of which help reveal what kind of animal was eaten.

Other signs*: Marsh rabbits create pathways through vegetation, as do many smaller animals. The width and location of these runways helps to determine what kind of animal uses them. There are recognizable differences in the mounds made by pocket gophers, moles, and certain insects. There are a variety of nests, such as the globular nest of the golden mouse, or nests built on platforms in the water by round-tailed muskrats. Other signs of animal activity include the burrows dug by armadillos, signs of rooting by feral hogs, and trees chewed by beavers.*

None of this is as thrilling as seeing a live animal in the wild. But a walk in the woods can be much more interesting with a little knowledge of the signs animals leave behind.

Otter

RIVER OTTER
(Lutra canadensis)

The river otter is common in all Florida waters except for true saltwater habitats. It is found in brackish river water as well as fresh water and also in salt marshes. This endearing, playful animal is well known for its method of entering the water by sliding down slippery river banks.

River otters were once found in all of North America, but now they are mainly found in the southeastern and northwestern United States, as well as the Great Lakes and Canada. Their decline began shortly after the arrival of the first European settlers on this continent, because their pelts were so highly valued. They have been completely eliminated from 11 states (and one Canadian province), primarily because of habitat destruction and water pollution, and they are rare in 13 more states. They were only recently reintroduced to the Great Smoky Mountains National Park, where they haven't been seen for the past 50 years. There are still plenty of river otters in Florida, though, from the Everglades all the way up through the Panhandle.

Otters are short-legged, aquatic carnivores, 3 to 4 feet long and from 12 to 30 pounds in weight. Nearly everything about them is adapted to an aquatic existence,

including their webbed feet, muscular tail, and cylindrical shape. While swimming under water, their heart slows to conserve oxygen, and valves over the nostrils and ears keep out water. An otter can stay under water 3 to 4 minutes on one breath. During this time it can swim about a quarter of a mile, at speeds up to 6 miles per hour, or dive up to 60 feet. An otter's hair is so thick, especially the oiled underfur, that its skin never gets wet.

Surprisingly, otters are not born with the ability to swim, even though they spend much of their lives in the water. They must be taught to swim by

their mother.

River otters are bank dwellers and live under the roots of trees at the water's edge. They do not excavate their own dens but use other animals' dens or natural holes. They may also build nests between the stones in seawalls and build little tunnels through the area.

Otters can detect movement through sensitive whiskers on the face which help them locate fish in murky water. Their hearing is well developed and otters communicate with each other with a variety of sounds. They probably have a good sense of smell which they use in communicating with other otters and in maintaining their territorial boundaries through scent marking. Otters are intelligent and have even been trained to capture and release fish and to retrieve waterfowl. Their sensitive whiskers are extremely important for catching fish in murky water, and the part of their brain dealing with touch and vibration is very highly developed.

Otters create their own "toilets," depositing most of their fecal material in one small area, and they use scent posts similar to those of a beaver to mark territory. (See the box on scent glands, page 37.) They clean their hair by rolling on the ground.

River otters are primarily diurnal (active during the day). They are most active from dawn until mid-morning and again around sunset. They spend about half their lives sleeping. A person would have to be quite lucky to see one sleeping in the wild, however.

Otters are social animals, although male otters are normally solitary. Before the pups are born, their father leaves home, and the female takes care of the babies by herself for the first eight weeks. The social group is the female and the pups from the previous breeding season.

Otters are one of over 100 mammals which have delayed implantation. Not until months

△ River otters are rarely seen sleeping in the daytime.

△ Surprisingly, river otters are not born with the ability to swim even though they spend much of their lives in the water. They must be taught by their parents.

△ The otter's food is fish, shellfish, crayfish, and frogs, plus some waterbirds. It has strong teeth capable of crushing bones, so when it eats an entire fish there is nothing left. Otters don't store food, and they don't overkill as do weasels and mink. They eat the fish that are the most abundant and easiest to catch. These are usually trash fish, so it is possible that otters benefit sport fish by reducing the fish that compete with sport fish. Many sport fishermen disagree, however, and despise otters, whom they see as competitors.

after fertilization does the egg implant in the uterus, but it is not known why this occurs.

Otters run on land by means of a peculiar doubling up and unfolding of the back. They tend to bounce as they move along. Many otters are killed by cars while crossing highways.

Otters' pelts are very valuable. Their fur is rated 100% on the fur quality scale. All other furs are judged in relation to an otter's fur. (The mole's fur is also highly rated by many authorities. Harvesting for pelts has had a great impact on otter populations at various times and places. But today the loss of otters is mainly caused by destruction of their habitat and changes in water quality.

The otter is a highly intelligent and curious animal. It is, like the dolphin, a rather playful animal. Because of its playfulness, it is one of the most popular animals at a zoo. Otters love to play games with each other and with people.

Otters are rarely handled by keepers at zoos or rehabilitation centers, however, because their teeth are so dangerous. Zookeepers who must handle an otter usually insist on giving it a tranquilizer shot first. An otter is not vicious and will not attack without reason or pursue a human, but it will not allow itself to be held without a fight.

Hand-raised otters love people, however, and especially dogs. Raccoons and otters also get along well. There's an otter on Pine Island that local people have raised that comes around when it's hungry, uses the swimming pool, and plays with the dogs.

BLACK BEAR
(Ursus americanus)

Black bears were formerly found throughout Florida except in the Florida Keys. Now they are localized in a few places. They are relatively common in the Big Cypress Swamp and Ocala National Forest and may also be seen occasionally in the Everglades and the northern counties of Florida, especially in riverine forests. Florida's bears are usually black with white markings but may also be brown. These are Florida's largest native land mammals (bison in Florida are all introduced).

Black bears are not "teddy bears" but very rugged, solitary, shy, and far-ranging mammals. They are found from Florida to Maine

△ Bears are good swimmers and in Florida use the water to keep cool in warm weather.

BEARS AND BEEKEEPERS

Florida is the number one honey producing state. Because black bears are particularly fond of honey and bee larvae and are fairly widespread in Florida, that spells trouble for beekeepers. A single bear may tear apart dozens of hives to get at the honey inside. Black bears with a sweet tooth have been responsible for destruction of beehives in 41 of the 43 counties in which they occur in Florida. To make matters worse, Florida's bears may remain active all year round, not hibernating as they would in cooler climates. Losses to bears are estimated to cost beekeepers $100,000 per year in Florida.

Beekeepers have fought back using a number of methods. Electric fences have been the most effective, but live trapping has also worked fairly well. Being trapped is so traumatic an experience for bears that they generally do not revisit the same hives after they are released. Over the years beekeepers have also illegally poisoned a number of bears.

and Alaska but once extended to Labrador and Mexico as well. Their range and numbers today are greatly reduced from former times, especially east of the Mississippi. These massive animals were hunted for food and clothing by Native Americans and even worshipped in some cultures.

Today there are an estimated 400 to 600 black bears in the Great Smoky Mountains National Park, some of the best remaining habitat in the eastern United States. Florida has the most widespread population of black bears in the southeastern United States, with between 500 and 1,000 in the entire state, although it is not known how many for sure.

Because black bears are secretive and usually inhabit densely vegetated areas, they are rarely seen in the wild, but to the trained eye they leave unmistakable signs of their presence. Bear tracks are easily identified, especially the rear prints which resemble human footprints in size and shape. Also sometimes seen are their scat (feces), signs of their feeding, and their beds or nests. They also leave teeth and claw marks about 5 feet off the ground on trees and poles, and some people think they make these marks to communicate with other bears.

Female black bears weigh 180 pounds; males may be much larger and occasionally reach 300 pounds or more. While some black bears reach 24 years of age, mortality is very high during the first two years of a bear's life, so the average life span is only seven years.

Bears have a terrific sense of smell and hearing but relatively poor sight. They love water and may swim to stay cool.

Black bears feed day and night, although they are most active at night or early morning. They love honey, berries,

△ Black bears easily climb trees and can jump to the ground from heights.

and many insects including honey bees, but their basic diet includes nuts, fruits, carrion, and just about anything they can get into their mouth. They are incredibly strong and can rip apart logs in search of insects. Bears eat fruits and the tender hearts of saw palmetto and cabbage palms, and consume acorns in great quantities in the fall. They also occasionally eat armadillos, wild hogs, and deer.

Black bears den in hollow trees or other cavities, but they more often make nests or beds on the ground for resting, birthing, and winter dormancy in Florida. They often nest in palmetto thickets, leaving a depression, sometimes lined with leaves, two to three feet across and about a foot deep. They also make nests of piled up leaves or pine needles which resemble enormous birds' nests.

In North Florida, black bears have a dormant period, called winter denning, but bears are not true hibernators. During denning, the bears' body temperature decreases, their metabolism and heart rate drops, and they lose about 25% of their weight. In the South they are easily aroused, however, and they move about when disturbed.

Bears mate in early summer and female bears give birth to twins, or occasionally triplets, in midwinter. Females with cubs mate every second year. The females build the

mounds in which the nests are made, but the males choose the location for the nests. The mother bear's milk is 10 times as rich as cow's milk. The cubs weigh from four to seven pounds when they first wander out of the den in May, but two years after birth they may weigh as much as 100 pounds. Their mothers guard the cubs for the first year or so, but when they are about 18 months old the cubs are driven off to fend for themselves.

Black bears usually range over 25 to 100 square miles and may travel as much as 20 miles in search of food or a mate. When two bears meet, a vicious fight often erupts, resulting in wounds and abscesses that would kill most large mammals, but the bears usually survive. A bear's greatest fear is a forest fire, which may send it fleeing in panic.

△ This black bear is eating insects. Bears feed mainly on plant matter, including herbs, grasses, fruit, and nuts, depending on the season. Only a small portion of their diet includes insects, and these are primarily insects that live in colonies and can be scooped up in large numbers, such as carpenter ants and bees.

△ Bears are very dangerous and should never be regarded as harmless, especially a sow with cubs. They should also never be fed, because feeding them causes the bears to lose their natural distrust of man. Bears nearly always get into trouble around people. Even though they have a natural fear of man in the woods, they often wander into campsites and towns, becoming a genuine nuisance.

HUNTING BEARS

Bears were hunted in Florida until 1993 for sport and for their fatty meat, which tastes like hamburger. There has been a legal hunting season in the Osceola National Forest in Columbia and Baker counties, about fifty miles west of Jacksonville, for years, even though bears were classified as threatened by the state of Florida and may soon be listed as endangered. The minimum legal size was increased recently from 100 to 200 pounds, because of the relatively small numbers of bears in the wild. Many environmentalists feel that they should not be hunted at all.

Black bear hunting in Florida was halted temporarily in 1993, and the ban may be made permanent. Advocates of bear hunting insist that the few areas where it was allowed have both enough bears and enough favorable habitat to sustain what they call, somewhat euphemistically, a "con-

trolled annual harvest."

Fortunately, on most occasions the hunters never saw a bear. Hunting was done with dogs trained to track bears. The dogs had to have enormous stamina, because bears can run great distances and will not climb trees or stand and fight unless they are tired. Bear hunting was thought to be one of the most dangerous outdoor activities (especially for the dogs), and the odds favored the bears. Nevertheless, about 50 bears were killed annually in Florida.

Black bears receive other sorts of protection in Florida. The buying or selling of bear parts, such as gall bladders (used by Chinese and Koreans in traditional medicine), or the bears themselves, is prohibited, and many people have been arrested for selling bear claw jewelry in Florida. Hunting is still permitted in some parts of the country

Raccoon

RACCOON
(Procyon lotor)

Chief Powhatan of the Algonquin Tribe, father of Pocahontas, called the raccoon "ah-coon-em." The settlers couldn't pronounce that, so they called it raccoon. Some say the name is derived from "arakun," Algonquin for "scratches with his hands." Because of its distinctive facial markings, the raccoon is also sometimes called a "masked bandit." More often it is simply called a "coon."

Florida's raccoons are much smaller than those in the North and the Midwest. It is a general rule of nature (with many exceptions) that within a given species, animals living closer to the equator are smaller than those further away. With more surface area per pound of body weight, smaller animals can dissipate heat more easily through their skin. Larger animals, on the other hand, can retain their body heat more readily in cold weather. Raccoons rarely weigh over 8 pounds in southern Florida, but with their long fur they usually look larger than they really are. In North Florida they may reach 10 or 15 pounds, and in the Midwest they grow as large as 30 or 40 pounds. One raccoon in Colorado weighed 62 pounds and was well over 4 feet long from its nose to the tip of its tail.

Raccoons are highly adaptable and are found in a number of different habitats in Florida where water is available, including swamps, pine forests, and mangroves. They sleep in trees (often cabbage palms) all day, but at night they come down out of their trees, head first, about an hour after dark, and start foraging for food.

Raccoons remain active all year in Florida. In northern climates they hole up for days at a time in the winter, but they do not go into true hibernation. A hollow tree is their preferred den.

A raccoon is thought to have a more acute sense of touch than a human. It has thousands more nerve endings in its forepaws than humans have in their hands, and the part of its brain that is used for tactile sensation is much larger and more developed than that of other, similarly sized mammals. This dexterity is useful for picking up small food items and for grasping food under water. Raccoons also have very keen hearing and sight. Although they are color blind, they have great night vision.

◁ Like dogs and cats and many other mammals, raccoons carry their young in their mouths when moving them from one nest to another.

RACCOONS AS PETS

Even though baby coons are very cute and gentle, they do not make good pets. When they grow up, they become extremely aggressive and uncontrollable.

Keeping wild animals as pets often causes problems. Keeping a raccoon as a pet may result in bites or the destruction of property by males reaching maturity and friends or neighbors bitten by a pet coon have to worry about rabies.

Raccoons were so popular at one time they were even kept as pets in the White House. Grace Coolidge, wife of President Calvin Coolidge, had a raccoon named Rebecca, and President Herbert Hoover had a raccoon named Susie. Each lived in the White House for the duration of that president's consecutive terms. It's no accident that both these raccoons were females. If they had been males and allowed to run free, they would have torn the White House apart unless they had been neutered. Today, pet raccoons in the White House would probably be viewed unfavorably by large numbers of the voting public.

A DISTINCTIVE HUMPED POSTURE

Note the distinctive peaked shape of the coon's back, with the head low and rump high. This is particularly noticeable when the animal is walking or running. The reason is that the raccoon's hind legs are much longer than its front legs. Also, the shape of the spine is a factor.

Raccoons often stand on their hind legs while using their front paws to manipulate food. Well developed hind limbs may be associated with their climbing ability.

When walking, the coon holds its tail lower than many other similar-sized animals.

Raccoons are alert, curious and intelligent, traits celebrated in native American folklore. After they have learned how to open a container, they remember how to do it for as long as a year without practicing. Raccoons have considerable ability in solving problems. They do at least as well as a cat, a fairly intelligent animal, and sometimes even better than apes and monkeys.

In Cape Sable, in the Everglades National Park, a researcher found seven "wells" dug by coons up to 20 inches deep. It is thought that these wells were used as a means of getting fresh drinking water. Coons also dig up sea turtle eggs from beaches and open alligator nests to get at their eggs.

Raccoons climb easily. They can jump from heights and land on their feet like a cat. They're great swimmers, swimming from key to key in the Florida Keys to prey on waterbirds nesting on the islands (although the birds probably suffer less predation from coons than they would if they nested on the mainland).

A raccoon can live as long as sixteen years in the wild. However, only one in a hundred lives for seven years in the wild, and most raccoons do not survive beyond two years. In juveniles, the main cause of death is lack of food. Baby coons are weaned at a very young age. When not well fed, they become vulnerable to intestinal parasites. Automobiles are probably the greatest cause of death among adults.

RACCOON BREEDING HABITS

Raccoons do not live together as mated pairs. The males mate with as many females as possible.

During the breeding season, females find a den. The male raccoon locates a female and, if she is willing, moves into her den for a short period of mating. Afterwards, the male resumes his wandering lifestyle.

When the young are born, the female cares for them and defends them. Raccoon mothers are unlikely to abandon their young even in the face of great danger.

The raccoon mother leaves the den only long enough to obtain food. She does not receive any help from the father, and in fact, would not accept any contact with a male raccoon during this period.

Raccoons are born with fur but are very helpless. Their eyes are closed at birth and do not open for several weeks. They don't even leave the den until they are eight to twelve weeks old. Raising young coons requires a great deal of effort by their mother.

Juvenile raccoons vocalize by chattering. Adults make similar sounds, but in deeper voices, including growls and barks.

Raccoon

△ In Florida, raccoons often spend the day resting in cabbage palms or hollow trees.

FEEDING COONS

It is unwise to feed raccoons because they can do lots of damage around a house, such as destroying bird feeders and digging up new plantings. Feeding them brings an abnormally high population of raccoons into the area, and they may tear at screens to get into houses for food. They are also likely to get into territorial battles. Raccoons fed by humans are more susceptible to disease and nutritional deficiencies than those on a natural diet. And there's always the threat that they might be carrying rabies.

NOT A GOOD IDEA!

RACCOONS AND RABIES

Raccoons in Florida are the number one carrier of rabies, and most of the human cases of rabies in Florida are from raccoons. Whenever a raccoon is found acting strangely, it should be assumed that it has rabies, even though canine distemper may cause similar behavior. It is important to avoid raccoons that are active during the day because they might be carrying rabies, especially those exhibiting abnormal behavior such as chewing, salivating, or drooling.

Rabies may take two forms in most animals, a furious form which causes its victim to become vicious and attack other animals, and a dumb form. The dumb form is more common with raccoons; the rabid animal simply acts dumb and bewildered and spends its time sitting around. It may sometimes chew its own tongue off.

Florida law requires the reporting of all animal bites to county health officials, whether it's by a dog or cat or a wild animal. In the case of a raccoon bite, an animal control officer will pay a friendly visit, kill the raccoon, and have it tested. In a typical situation in Charlotte County recently, a man tried to break up a fight between his dog and a raccoon. The raccoon bit both the dog and the man. It was destroyed and found to have rabies. A coon with rabies cannot travel very far, so it is generally easy to follow, but its capture should be left to professionals.

Raccoons seem cute to humans and always stir a lot of attention and interest. Their appearance (the face mask), their ability to use their hands in a human-like way, their curiosity and intelligence, and their slow, waddling manner of walking are among the traits that many people find appealing.

The raccoon is one of the most versatile animals. A raccoon can exist alongside humans and in human-modified habitats. Because of this tolerance, raccoons are among the mammals that will probably survive if Florida eventually becomes wall-to-wall development.

There are a number of reasons for the raccoons' ability to survive in these unnatural conditions. Raccoons eat a wide range of food and can use many different kinds of homesites, ranging from a culvert to a treetop. Their intelligence has helped them adapt to new and ever-changing conditions.

△ Coons are able to use almost every type of habitat, from urban to rural, including both uplands and swamps.

△ Raccoons are intelligent enough to open most storage containers including garbage cans and backpacks. Some Florida subdivisions require raccoon-proof garbage cans.

Raccoons are opportunistic feeders and eat just about anything including berries, fruits, plants, fish and crabs, beetles, mice, and carrion. These "masked bandits" have a habit of raiding garbage cans in picnic areas. They also clean out bird feeders and break into chicken coops in search of chickens and their eggs. If a camper leaves his supplies unattended, a raccoon does not even have to put on a mask to carry out the robbery.

△ Baby orphan coons at a rehabilitation center are fed a special formula with a medicine dropper.

◁ Raccoon eating a turtle.

◁ Coons are called "masked bandits" because of the trademark black "mask" across their eyes and their tendency to steal food from campers and farmers.

△ This coon is not an albino but an unusually light color phase. Other normally colored coons in the same colony treated this individual as an outcast.

▽ In this photo, the baby pet raccoons are following their owner. Raccoons are social animals, and, like dogs, which are also social animals, raccoons tend to identify with the person who raised them.

DO RACCOONS REALLY WASH THEIR FOOD?

It is a myth that raccoons always wash their food before eating it. The raccoon's species name, lotor, means washer, because raccoons were once thought to wash their food, but this is largely incorrect. Raccoons do spend much of their lives around ponds and streams, but most of the photos of raccoons holding food over water actually show raccoons harvesting food from the water. Raccoons obtain much of their food by using their paws to search underwater around rocks and crevices for small fish, frogs, and crayfish. Raccoons have considerable ability to identify, hold, and manipulate these food items with their dexterous front paws. Another related myth is that raccoons must wet their food because they lack salivary glands, but this has been proven to be simply a folktale.

COON HUNTING

The coonskin cap associated with Davy Crockett, which included the coon's distinctively ringed tail, is an important element of American folklore. The raccoon pelt was valuable to the early soldiers, settlers, and frontiersmen, and even today it is still used for clothing, although much less frequently. Consequently, trapping and hunting is still a cause of raccoon mortality. However, today there is more awareness of the cruelty involved to both the raccoons and the dogs.

Using dogs to tree raccoons at night is an old southern tradition. Coons are not generally hunted for food but for their pelts. Until recently, a coon pelt was worth $40 to $60 dollars. But now they are almost worthless, as the market for genuine fur has declined due to pressure from animal-rights activists.

Coon hunting is still quite popular in Florida, especially in rural areas. An experienced coon hunter hopes to kill 10 to 15 coons in a single

night. Florida, like most of the south, is excellent coon-hunting territory. There is no closed season for coon hunting, and farmers sometimes pay hunters a bounty because they consider the animals a nuisance. Coons like to nest in barns, and they contaminate cattle feed with their feces. They also chew holes in barns and present the threat of rabies.

Raccoons are hunted at night using hounds. The dogs follow the distinctive scent trail of the coon. The raccoon runs until he gets tired and then climbs a tree. When the dogs find the tree which the raccoon has climbed, they stay there and bark until the hunters arrive and shoot the coon or call the hounds off and let the coon go. The raccoon will hurt the dogs if their handlers allow contact. Raccoons can out-fight any dog pound for pound but cannot defeat an entire pack of dogs.

RABIES

Rabies was one of the first diseases known to be transmitted from animals to man. Rabies is a Latin word derived from an old Sanskrit word which means "to do violence." The first reference to rabies appeared in the Samarian code at about 1885 B.C. which mentioned "...mad dogs which bite people causing death."

Rabies is a viral nerve disease which generally begins with the bite of an infected animal. After the bite occurs, the virus moves up the neurons (the nerve cells) toward the brain. Usually, no symptoms are noticed during this incubation period until the virus hits certain areas of the brain. Then the clinical signs appear and shortly thereafter the person or animal dies. Death usually occurs from paralysis of the diaphragm, which stops respiration. About the same time that it reaches the brain, the virus also moves into the salivary glands, and thereafter it can be transmitted by saliva, through bites.

Different individuals respond to the virus in different ways and show different symptoms. Fear of water is a common symptom—rabies is also known as hydrophobia—but not always present. Rabies is almost always fatal in humans once the clinical signs appear. There are only 3 documented cases of survival.

In the United States, rabies was first observed in Virginia in 1753. By 1990 it had been recorded throughout the country. Since 1881, there have been a total of 73 human cases of rabies reported in Florida, the last one in 1948.

Rabies in dogs and cats, people, and wildlife are all interrelated. Rabies passing from person to person is almost nonexistent. People usually get rabies only as a result of being bitten by a rabid animal.

Up until the 1950s, humans acquired rabies mostly from dogs, but the availability of a rabies vaccine for dogs completely changed the situation. Louis Pasteur, of pasteurized milk fame, is the inventor of the rabies vaccine for dogs. In the late '40s and early '50s, local governments in the United States made a great effort to vaccinate dogs for rabies. The lack of human cases from dog bites in recent years is a tribute to the success of this campaign. However, people are not vaccinating pet cats, which may encounter rabid wild animals. Most Florida counties require vaccinations for both cats and dogs, but this is not the law everywhere.

Since most dogs have been vaccinated, the greatest danger of rabies today is from wild animals. Most cases arise from the bites of raccoons, foxes, bats, and skunks. In Florida, most of the bites are from raccoons. Unfortunately, wild animal pets cannot be vaccinated, because there is no licensed vaccine for these animals in the United States. This is one of many good reasons for not keeping wild animals as pets.

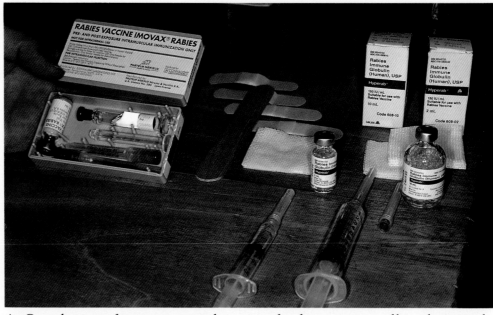

△ Complete set of instruments and vaccines for the treatment of bites by animals suspected of being rabid.

Rabies is generally passed via infected saliva, when people are bitten by animals. However, an animal with rabies which does not yet have the virus in its saliva cannot transmit the disease through its bite. In general, only infected animals showing symptoms of rabies have the virus in their saliva and are capable of transferring the disease, but there are exceptions. A skunk may have the virus in its saliva for months before it shows any signs of rabies.

Although virtually all rabies cases are acquired through saliva, there have been some unusual cases in which skunks passed the virus through the mother's milk. Rabies can possibly be acquired by inhaling the air in bat caves, but this mode of transmission has not been confirmed.

About 100 cases of rabies are identified in wild animals each year in Florida. Most animals tested are near populated areas, where the risk to pets and humans is greatest, so the actual incidence of rabies in the wild is unknown. As with people, a wild mammal rarely recovers once the rabies symptoms have begun.

The time from exposure, or being bitten by a rabid animal, until the disease appears can be up to 2 years. Each species of animal, including man, has a different incubation period. The average incubation period for man is 100 days or less, and most animals, including man, develop the disease a few months after exposure. However, the length of the incubation period also depends on the location of the bite. If the bite is on the face or head, the disease may appear within a few weeks. If a toe is bitten, it is far less likely that the disease will appear at all and if it does, it might take 6 months to a year. Because of its long incubation period, rabies is the only virus disease presently known which can be prevented by a vaccine taken after exposure.

There are 2 types of rabies: a dumb form and a furious form. The victims of the furious form, mostly dogs, often exhibit biting and snapping behavior and become very aggressive. Hydrophobia, a fear of water, is also present. The dumb form is the form most common to cattle. The victims of the dumb form rarely attack, but they behave abnormally. A rabid fox or raccoon, for example, may walk about in daylight, a very uncharacteristic behavior for these nocturnal animals.

All mammals can get rabies, but the susceptibility of species varies enormously. Foxes are very susceptible to rabies, followed by skunks, cats, raccoons, and bats, and then cattle, man, horses, and dogs. Almost all the cases of fox rabies in Florida have been in the northern part of the state.

The first case of rabies in a raccoon in Florida was discovered in 1947, the first case in bats in 1953. Its spread among raccoons throughout the state was not documented until the 1970s. Three different bat species carry rabies, the yellow bat being the most common. In some areas of the United States, skunks show the highest incidence of rabies among the animals tested.

Some mammals, such as opossums, seem highly resistant to rabies, or have not yet been documented as vulnerable. Rabies also appears to be very uncommon in rodents. Since 1957, thousands of squirrels, rats, and mice have been examined, and only one was found to be rabid. There is no known case of a person getting rabies from a rodent's bite. Rabies has never been documented in birds.

WHAT TO DO IF A WILD ANIMAL BITES YOU?

In the United States, 20,000 people are treated each year for exposure to rabies. The injections are no longer as painful an ordeal for the patient as they used to be.

If an animal is suspected of having rabies, and it has bitten someone or caused alarm in some way, the first thing to do is to call Animal Control so that they can kill or capture the animal. If the animal has to be killed to be captured, the head must not be destroyed, because the brain tissue has to be examined. The tissue cannot be frozen but must be refrigerated. Anyone touching the animal should use gloves to avoid contact with its saliva.

When diagnosing rabies in animals, the brain tissue is examined, so the animal must be sacrificed. A pathological examination is conducted to determine whether or not the animal had rabies by examining the brain for black spots (negri bodies) and through antibody tests. If it is determined that the animal which has bitten a person has rabies, complex decisions must be made about the course of treatment. Without any treatment, the probability of getting rabies after exposure is less than 1% for a minor wound, but over 50% for a deep puncture wound near the head.

Veterinarians and other people that may be exposed to rabid animals, such as wildlife officers and animal control officers, are periodically vaccinated against rabies as a precautionary measure

▷ The series of rabies vaccine injections is now given in the arm rather than in the stomach, as was the practice in the past. The treatment now is not nearly so difficult or painful as it was years ago.

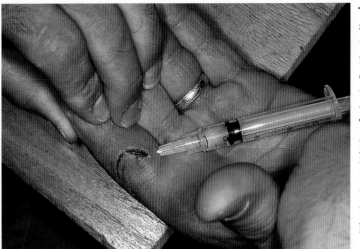

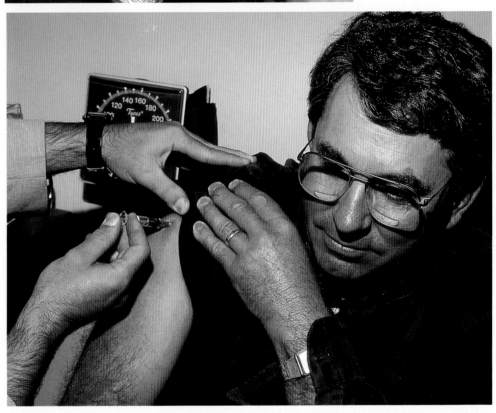

◁ One of the first steps in the modern treatment of bites from suspected rabies carriers is to inject the site of the wound with the rabies serum. The serum works immediately to start killing the virus. This is important because the vaccine takes up to 60 days to build a person's immunity.

RABIES IN THE RECENT PAST

The following historical account gives a vivid description, in the colorful language of that period, of the course of "hydrophobia," or rabies, in humans: A Dr. Lancaster of Gainesville wrote a letter to the editor in 1894, which was the first report of a human case of rabies in Florida:

"Having recently been called up to treat a case of hydrophobia, rabies, ... On the 27th of last July, Margaret Anderson, a colored woman, age 57 years, was bitten by a sick cat. The animal's teeth went into the fleshy part of the hand and holding on until pried lose. Four days later I was called and found an extensive cellulitis on the hand which I incised, liberating pus. I ordered the hand poulticized with carbonized flaxseed and ... in the course of time the hand returned to its normal condition. On the 19th of November, I was called again and found the patient in a nervous condition with an ill-defined dread manifesting itself with a constant change of positioning and in the appealing look and words of the patient to do something for her relief. She complained of a stiffening of the hand and arm accompanied by shooting pains extending from the hand to the shoulder. I at once recognized the symptoms of hydrophobia. I offered water to the patient. However, there was some difficulty in swallowing. This symptom increased until the sight or even mention of water brought on painful laryngeal contractions with the expression of fear and pain and the patient longed to have it removed from sight. There was an indescribable wild, scared look about the patient with constant restlessness ... The attempt to give .. other remedies brought on such paroxysms of fear and pain that I gave her no remedies other than hypodermic injections of morphine and atropia. This I gave for controlling the suffering. The patient died on the 20th, some 48 hours after the first decided symptoms. At no time did the patient attempt to harm her attendants or was there any attempt to mimic the bark of a dog or cry of a cat. Though there was a frequent reference to the cat bite by the patient who clearly recognized her trouble and the unfavorable prognosis. There was a constant dripping from her mouth of ... saliva, obstinate constipation and inability to swallow liquids or solids the last 24 hours of life."

Note: Dr. Lancaster's method of diagnosis (offering the patient water and observing her distress) was commonly practiced many years ago. However it is now known that different individuals respond to the virus in different ways and show different symptoms. Fear of water is not always present.

Skunks

STRIPED SKUNK
(*Mephitis mephitis*)

Well known for its scent, the striped skunk is found from Canada to Northern Mexico and in all 48 contiguous states. It is found throughout Florida, including the Keys. The word skunk comes from the Algonquin Indian name for these animals, "segonku." They are also sometimes called polecats, but true polecats are European animals more closely related to the domesticated ferret.

Skunks can live in a wide variety of habitats. Since they are comfortable around humans, somewhat like deer and squirrels, skunks can often survive in towns and cities, including New York City. They occasionally live in or under buildings. If people with skunks living under their home object to their odor, the skunks can be chased away with moth balls. They are, however, useful in eating insect pests. Some people keep skunks as pets. This is unwise because they often carry rabies.

The striped skunk is a slow moving animal. It seldom climbs, unlike the spotted skunk, which is a good climber. It can swim short distances. The hearing and sight of skunks is poor to fair.

Striped skunks are considered friends by farmers because of the great numbers of mice and insects they kill. However, skunks are misunderstood and disliked by many people because they present a danger from rabies and because of their foul-smelling spray.

Like raccoons, skunks are nocturnal and omnivorous. They spend the entire night eating everything they can get their paws on.

△ The classic color of the striped skunk is two white stripes that meet on the head, but colors vary from almost all white to almost all black. The more common form is more black than white.

Striped skunks eat mice, young birds, nuts, fruits, eggs, and garbage, but they generally consume more insects than everything else. They normally get very fat during the summer and utilize the fat during the winter months, even in Florida.

Skunks live in burrows, often those of other animals such as the armadillo. They are mostly asocial and solitary, but, in the North, females sometimes winter together (biologists do not completely understand this behavior) in cozy underground dens, hollow tree trunks, or perhaps even under houses or barns. In the South, skunks remain active year round. During the mating season, in spring, the males sometimes fight, and they may even spray one another. After mating, the male leaves the female.

Females give birth two months after mating to 4 to 8 blind, hairless kittens, sometimes more. They usually have one or two litters a year and can nurse 6 kittens at one time; in larger litters the weakest kittens usually starve. The young can spray at around 2 to 4 weeks of age, when their eyes first open. Young skunks first leave the den, after dark, when they are about 6 weeks old, and totter behind their mother single file. Every night they follow approximately the same route.

The mother skunks are very maternal. They teach their young how to hunt and how to defend themselves, They may even adopt and raise orphaned skunk kittens.

Striped skunks have a narrow white stripe from their nose to their forehead which usually splits into two stripes that run along their sides. These distinctive markings help other animals learn to recognize skunks and leave them alone. The bold, black and white pattern is a danger warning.

Skunks are important for their pelts in the north. Their fur is sleek and glossy. Among trappers, white on the head only is called a star, a stripe back to the hips is called a half-stripe, and white the full length of the abdomen and the tail is called a white skunk, the most valuable

for pelts. Their hair color varies from cream to black, and browns also occur. Occasionally a striped skunk may be silver, with a faint stripe, or pure albino, with no stripe, but these variation are rather rare.

Because they are curious and not too wary, skunks are easily trapped. Their fur has been sold as "Alaskan sable" or "black marten" and at one time was highly valued by trappers. When a law requiring honest labeling went into effect, sales went way down, however, and trapping declined. It seems that skunk fur, labeled as such, didn't have nearly as much appeal.

Great horned and barred owls prey on skunks as do foxes and bobcats. Unlike other animals, however, the owl, if sprayed, seems not to notice. Because skunks are often found on roads at night feeding on dead snakes and frogs, automobiles also are a major cause of death.

Skunks, like most other mammals, can be infected with rabies, but the incidence of rabies in skunks varies yearly and from one region to another. In Florida, rabies is on the rise, but can be transmitted by a range of potential hosts, including raccoons, skunks and foxes, but also feral cats and dogs.

Skunks

SPOTTED SKUNK (*Spilogale putorius*)

The spotted skunk is much smaller than the striped skunk. It is about the size of a squirrel, while the striped skunk is about as big as a house cat. The spotted skunk is actually striped with one large spot between the eyes and four stripes down its back, but the stripes are wavy and broken and appear like spots. Its markings help warn off its enemies in the day and help the skunk hide at night.

Like the striped skunk, the spotted skunk is nocturnal, and it is very elusive, so it is seldom seen. If one appears during the day, that is out of character and an indication that it might have rabies.

Spotted skunks are excellent climbers. They climb trees, buildings, barns, and chicken coops. Their principal foods are insects, especially beetles, but they eat plant material, and they are good mousers and eat other small animals as well. They are especially fond of chickens and other poultry. These are the most predatory of all skunks. They will even steal small mammals from traps.

The spotted skunk's Latin name means "stinking spotted weasel," and this skunk is sometimes known as the weasel skunk. It is also called civet cat, although it differs from the true African civet cat.

Spotted skunks mate in the spring. In Florida they may produce two litters a year. At about 6 weeks of age the babies start following their mom around in a line. Their main enemies are farm dogs and owls.

◁ Baby skunks have the colors of the adults. They are already spotted at birth.

Spotted skunks need a dry habitat. They are found in northwestern Florida and from the central peninsula southward. They live in flatwoods and mixed scrub, in dark, well-protected, underground dens. They sometimes use the burrows of gophers.

Before the Great Depression, spotted skunks were common around small farms in the Midwest where mice were abundant. As the small farms disappeared, however, the skunks disappeared also.

Today, one of the largest known populations of spotted skunks in North America is found on the Cape Canaveral National Seashore. These skunks have been studied since 1982. They eat rodents

△ Spotted skunks climb trees to escape their enemies on the ground.

and reptiles, den up in gopher tortoise burrows, and require almost no drinking water to survive. Saw palmetto provides cover that helps protect the skunks from great horned owls and barred owls.

THE SKUNK'S POWERFUL SCENT

When a skunk is confronted, it arches its back and stamps or shuffles its front feet in an attempt to scare off the threatening animal. It sometimes also hisses. If that doesn't work, a spotted skunk will rear up on its front legs in a handstand, its hind legs in the air and its tail straight up or curled over its back, making the skunk appear much larger. If the attacker does not heed these warnings, the skunk will then release a foul-smelling stream of musk from its anal glands. Sometimes a skunk will spray while doing the handstand, but more often it squirts only after returning to all four legs, with its body twisted into a U-shape so it can see its enemy as it sprays.

The spray comes from anal glands surrounded by muscles. The gland ducts, one on each side of the anus, protrude like small nozzles when the skunk is threatened or angry. The skunk fires by contracting the muscles around these glands. Each gland has a sack which holds about a tablespoonful of a yellowish, oily liquid. Either atomized spray or larger droplets come out. The spray does not get on the skunk itself.

Skunks only spray in self-defense. The first discharge is the strongest, but they are capable of about 5 or 6 shots before running out of fluid. In a few hours they can fire again, and in a few days they are completely replenished.

Skunks are quite accurate from about 6 feet and fairly accurate up to 10 feet. They aim at the attacker's face and usually hit

their target. The liquid burns the eyes and may cause temporary blindness, but it has no permanent effect.

The spray clings to whatever it touches, and the smell can last for weeks. Butylmercaptain, the active ingredient, can be detected half a mile or more downwind.

Skunks can spray while held by the tail. To prevent them from spraying, skunks are held with a hand around their neck and their tail tucked up under their rear.

Vinegar, stale beer, tomato juice, or baking

soda will help remove the skunk's odor. Washing with ammonia or tomato juice is the most commonly used remedy, but the best method, according to some folks, is to bury the clothes for a week, dig them up, wash them thoroughly in vinegar, and then throw them away!

Small amounts of skunk or civet musk are used in some of the world's most expensive perfumes. These tiny amounts of musk help the perfumes hold their fragrance much longer.

Mink

MINK
(Mustela vison)

The mink is a close relative of the long-tailed weasel and, like other members of the genus *mustela*, has a long thin body and short legs. However, mink are larger than weasels.

Mink are bank dwellers. They would rather occupy the homes of other animals than make their own. They are considered semi-aquatic. They have partially webbed feet and spend more time close to water than weasels. They eat fish, while weasels generally do not.

Mink and weasels are both animals which have been hunted for their pelts, and this hunting is regulated by the state of Florida. It is illegal to take mink in Florida, and weasels are seldom seen. Furthermore, with the price at about one dollar a pelt for weasels, and only a little more for mink, they're not worth trapping. Most fur-bearing animals do not develop a valuable, dense undercoat in Florida because of the warm climate.

Mink eat mammals, fish, and frogs, among other things. They are capable of hunting on land as well as in the water.

Mink are rare in Florida. Their distribution in this state is closely tied to the drainage of wetlands and to development. They are found most typically in the marshes of the Big Cypress region, although they do occur in sawgrass areas. The Everglades mink is an endangered population.

△ Minks live around water. They swim and dive to catch fish, frogs, and crayfish but will eat small mammals as well.

◁ Note the distinctive white marking under the chin which appears on many, but not all, Florida mink.

LONG-TAILED WEASEL
(Mustela frenata)

Weasels are rare and very seldom seen in Florida. They are more common in northern states. Weasels are sparsely distributed throughout much of Florida, but are absent from the southeast portion of the state. Their low numbers and their shy, elusive nature make it difficult for scientists to study them.

The weasel uses the burrows of other animals. It climbs trees very reluctantly. It is strictly a meat-eater, and feeds chiefly on rodents, including pocket gophers, wood rats, and cotton mice. However, it will eat nearly anything that moves, including mammals larger than itself, such as rabbits, in addition to birds, lizards, and frogs. It is especially fond of poultry, and if it gets into a coop it may kill many chickens, in a frenzy, without feeding on any. It can squeeze through very small cracks to get into buildings. There are very few places a small mammal can go that a weasel cannot follow.

Weasels have insatiable curiosity, and they are constantly in motion. They are difficult to photograph and difficult to trap.

Weasels are found in a variety of habitats in Florida but are associated most often with forests and agricultural fields, probably because of the availability of prey. They are considered protected, fur-bearing animals by the state of Florida.

▷ Weasels stand tall to look for prey as well as to keep an eye out for danger. They run into their holes in the ground to escape predators.

TRAPPING

There is still some trapping in Florida, but on a much smaller scale than in the past. The sale of pelts still probably generates a half million dollars a year for trappers. Raccoons are the most commonly trapped animals, followed by otters and bobcats. Smaller numbers of beavers and coyotes are also trapped in Florida.

Leg-hold traps, the most inhumane method of trapping, are illegal in Florida as in most other states. The newer, live traps are far more humane, because the trapper can kill the animal swiftly rather than allowing it to be maimed and left to suffer for a long time.

Pressure from animal rights groups along with the availability of inexpensive substitute fabrics has greatly decreased the demand for fur. Prices of pelts have fallen greatly, and, as a result, few people now engage in mammal trapping.

Deer

WHITE-TAILED DEER
(Odocoileus virginianus)

The white-tailed deer is one of the most highly adaptable animals in the New World (Western Hemisphere). Its range extends from Hudson Bay in Canada through the United States to Central and South America, from jungles to high mountain areas. It is absent in Utah and rare in Nevada and California, however.

Sixteen subspecies of white-tailed deer are found from Canada through South America, and they vary considerably in size. These deer can range from as large as 400 pounds for a big buck in northern states to as little as 45 to 55 pounds for Florida's key deer.

White-tailed deer are beautiful, shy creatures who move with great agility and grace. They are named for the white undersurface of the tail, which is displayed as a flag when the animal bounds off. Their speed, excellent sense of smell, and keen ears are their main defenses against predators.

▷ This photo shows the white underside of the tail. The tail is raised when the deer is alarmed. The raised white tail may be a danger signal to alert the other deer in the herd. Deer also communicate by stamping and snorting, and by glandular secretions rubbed on vegetation and the ground.

Most large herbivores are primarily either browsers or grazers, although many do both on occasion. Animals that are browsers, such as deer, eat shrubs, bushes, and the bark of trees. Grazers, like cows, typically eat grasses. White-tailed deer can adapt to different terrain and different food supplies. They are strictly herbivores, but they eat a wide range of plants. Mast, composed of fallen acorns, nuts, and fruits, is an important source of high-protein food for deer. Deer drink both fresh water and some salt water, but they cannot survive on salt water alone.

HOW THEY SURVIVE ON BARK AND LEAVES

Deer are ruminants, like cows, with a four-chambered stomach. They chew their cud, bringing food up for more chewing. Ruminants can eat roughage such as leaves or bark which is non-digestible to humans and other mammals that have simple stomachs. This fiber is then broken down by cellulose-loving bacteria which live in the stomach of the ruminant. The bacteria are passed down the digestive tract and absorbed as nutrients. So the ruminant animal actually lives mostly on bacteria!

◁ Deer fawns have spotted coats like baby panthers (see photo in box at left). The spots may provide camouflage for the young while they are most vulnerable.

Deer

△ Antlers showing velvet.

HORNS AND ANTLERS

Horns and antlers function as weapons and also make an animal appear larger to a potential opponent. They may also play a role in sexual attraction.

Unlike antlers, horns are not shed; they ordinarily last a lifetime (except those of the pronghorn antelope, found in the western United States). Horn growth produces rings, like a tree, but unlike trees, the rings of a horn are visible on the outside of the horn. Horns are not naturally hollow. There is a core of bone and soft tissue inside. The bison is an example of an animal with horns. Indians and pioneers used hollowed-out bison horns to store their gunpowder.

Horn tips are often removed from domestic animals to keep them from hurting each other and to make them less dangerous to humans. If the tip of a horn is cut off, the animal will bleed a lot from the soft tissue inside. Cutting a horn is also very painful for the animal. Ranchers now use hot irons to slice off the tips of the horns of domestic animals. This stops the bleeding but is still painful. Some new breeds today are "polled," meaning hornless.

In contrast to horns, antlers are shed and replaced every year. Antlers begin to grow in the spring. In the fall, they become tough and hard as they cease to grow, and the deer begin scratching them against trees and brush, sharpening the tines (points) and removing the velvet. This is the beginning of the rut (the breeding season), when the males become more aggressive. The antlers are shed in the fall after the breeding season, up to late winter in Florida, and grow back again the following year. They pop off with slight bleeding.

THE VELVET

Antlers grow from bones of the skull and are covered by velvet, a soft, skin-like tissue which grows on the antlers. Velvet is very rich in blood and is warm to the touch.

Only male white-tailed deer have antlers, plus perhaps one out of 100,000 females, but female antlers are not shed annually. A deer has only small antlers (tiny buttons or spikes) its first year. This first year deer is called a yearling or a spike buck. Its first full set of antlers is usually seen at 16 to 18 months. Each year the new set of antlers becomes larger until full size is reached after five to six years.

Nutrition plays a large role in the size of the antlers and is even more important than genetics. In particular, the amount of calcium and phosphorus in the soil helps determine the size of the antlers. A poor diet results in antlers which are smaller than those of previous years.

Deer antlers (along with many other deer parts) are harvested in some places for use in Chinese medicine. Whole antlers are sold in Asian medical shops. Customers slice them and boil them with chicken to make a tonic.

THE RUT

As soon as the antlers stop growing and the velvet dries up, the deer rubs it off against trees and brush. This helps build up strength in the deer's neck muscles for jousting, and it stirs up hormones in the males that incite them to fight one another for females. This is the start of the breeding season called the rut.

Fighting among the male deer becomes intense. Sometimes two males lock antlers and cannot separate. When this happens, they may both starve to death. An area about a hundred yards wide may be completely trampled during the struggle of the two animals. Male deer in rut are so aggressive that they sometimes charge people. This is one of the dangers of raising an orphaned male fawn in captivity.

96

SPIKE BUCKS

Normally, antlers drop off each year in late fall after the rut (breeding season) and are regrown again during spring and summer in time for the next year's rut. A spike buck is a yearling with its first antlers, which usually have just one point (photo below). The second-year antlers usually have two points, the third-year usually three. After three years (as in photo at left), the number of points is variable and depends on both age and nutrition.

△ A deer with three antlers walking through wamp. When the germinal tissue has been injured, the rack of antlers becomes deformed, increasingly so every year. These unusual racks are especially desired by trophy-seeking hunters.

LICKING BEHAVIOR

This deer is licking the side of a cypress tree, probably for minerals as a supplement to its usual diet. Deer also sometimes lick ashes after a fire, presumably for the same reason.

Deer are known for their licking behavior. They have been seen licking the sides of painted barns and even licking grease from tractor engines. The reason for this strange behavior is not known.

Deer

White-tailed deer like to travel in groups which include several females with their offspring. The bucks usually live separately. It is unusual among mammals for adults to play, but among white-tailed deer, adults as well as the young like to kick and play.

The major predator of deer in earlier times was the mountain lion, but today it is man. Dogs may kill 10 percent of the legal harvest in some states, a very large number. Coyotes, wolves, and bobcats also kill some deer. In states such as Florida where there are panthers, deer are one of their main foods. The deer's excellent sense of smell is one of its main defenses against these predators.

White-tailed deer may become very tolerant of people if not disturbed, and they seem to thrive where land has been cleared. They are a problem for farmers because they like to eat cultivated crops and can do considerable damage to corn or grains, apples, vineyards, soybeans, and other crops. In Florida they are a problem for citrus growers. They damage tree farms as well. They have become a major management problem in some areas.

◁ Deer can easily jump over most agricultural fences. Grove owners need to keep deer out of their orange groves because the deer eat the buds and young leaves from the orange trees. Deer fences need to be 8 to 10 feet high.

▽ Some Florida ranchers feed wild deer around their farm buildings, just because they like to see them near their homes.

THE MOST DANGEROUS ANIMAL IN AMERICA?

Deer cause more human deaths than any other animal in the United States. They often cross roads at night, and they tend to freeze when they see approaching headlights. The resulting collisions cause many human fatalities. In some states, more deer are killed by motor vehicle collisions than by legal hunting.

DEER "SCRAPES"

White-tailed deer have four sets of scent glands: the preorbitals in the corners of their eyes, (which also produce tears), metatarsals on the outside of the hind legs between the ankle and the hoof, tarsals on the inside of the hind legs, and the interdigitals between the toes. These scent glands are used for marking territory, They are cut out when meat is dressed to prevent the oily smell from contaminating the meat.

Male white-tailed deer (bucks) mark their territory by creating "scrapes." They paw an area, urinate on it, and apply material from their scent glands. Many other mammals also mark territory with their scent. These markings usually warn other males to "keep out," and help males and females locate each other.

DEER HUNTING AND MANAGEMENT

White-tailed deer are the most popular big game animals in the United States. Schools used to close the first day of the hunting season in some areas. About 80,000 deer are shot legally ("harvested") every year in Florida. The illegal harvest is believed to exceed the legal harvest in many states. Half the deer killed in the United States are killed illegally.

Hunting generally is on the decline, but there are still many millions of deer hunters in the United States. In Pennsylvania, it is thought that the hunters outnumber the deer that may be legally killed.

Game conservation and management is devoted to maintaining a population that is in balance with the ability of the land to support it. Overpopulation causes deer to become scrawny and more susceptible to parasites. Where overpopulated, the deer over-browse and overgraze. Cougars and wolves, the primary predators in the past, helped keep the deer populations under control, but these natural predators are much more scarce today than they once

were. Consequently, white-tailed deer populations are thought to exceed the optimal carrying capacity of the land in most states.

In Florida, the deer population today is at an all-time high, a remarkable recovery from 50 or 60 years ago when there were only about 20,000 deer in the entire state, and a tribute to the management programs which were adopted. Protection from poaching was a major factor. Now there are about 900,000 deer just in Florida, more than there were east of the Mississippi in 1900.

Deer populations can be manipulated by controlling hunting seasons and rules (bag limits), managing habitats, and managing people and illegal poaching. The deer's primary habitat is forests and adjacent farm lands, and this habitat is still being lost to development in many areas.

Deer were a major source of food for American Indians thousands of years ago. Artifacts made of deer bones have been found in Native American archaeological sites throughout North America.

Because of their popularity as hunting animals, deer have been more closely studied from a game management perspective than any other species in North America. Some deer are kept for purposes of photography. They are fed well and given hormones so they will grow unusually large racks of antlers.

KEY DEER
(*Odocoileus virginianus clavium*)

Florida's key deer, a subspecies of the white-tailed deer, is the smallest native deer in North America. These deer have been nicknamed "toy deer" because of their small size. Key deer are on the average smaller than the mainland deer, but size varies. All deer in Florida tend to be smaller than deer from the northern states. Key deer are found almost entirely on two of the Florida Keys, Big Pine and No Name, with most of the animals on Big Pine Key. Formerly they were found on some of the other keys as well.

Key Deer populations were once much larger, but poaching and dogs almost wiped them out. Their trusting, gentle nature proved to be unfortunate for the deer, because it made them an easy target for poachers. They were down to an estimated 26 individuals in 1945.

Key deer were probably saved from extinction by a cartoon which showed the tiny deer being harassed by poachers and dogs. This cartoon was the work of "Ding" Darling, a nationally syndicated political cartoonist who loved and respected nature, and who is also known for helping to establish the wildlife refuge on Sanibel Island that bears his name. The National Key Deer Refuge on Big Pine Key was founded in 1957 as a result of this cartoon, and the deer population has now increased to about 250 to 300. Inbreeding in so small a population is still a serious problem, however. It can lead to lower success at reproduction, greater vulnerability to disease, and a generally less healthy population.

The Key deer is listed as endangered by both the Florida Game and Fresh Water Fish Commission and the U.S. Fish and Wildlife Service. Poaching continued until the 1980s at the rate of 5 to 10 deer per year, but automobiles and habitat loss due to development are the greatest threats to the deer today, although poaching still occurs. Cruel poachers reportedly killed one tame key deer with a hammer. Automobiles still kill more than 50 key deer each year; 862 key deer were killed on roads from 1970 through 1988. Fawns occasionally drown in drainage ditches, and some deer are still killed by dogs or chased by dogs onto roads where they are struck by cars.

OH, DEER!

Many tourists and residents fed the deer in the past, but this brought them closer to roads, where they were more vulnerable to cars, and it may have also increased the chance of disease. Feeding was made illegal in 1982, but it is difficult to halt it completely. Some key deer still expect to be hand fed, and some are nuisances.

Key deer drink salt water once in a while for its salt content, but they cannot survive on it. Their existence in the Keys depends on the availability of fresh water. They swim well and may travel from one island to another in search of food. They were hunted at least as far back as 400 years ago and were even harpooned in the water by sailors.

△ Key deer eating mangrove leaves. Key deer are both grazers (feeding on grasses) and browsers (feeding on shrubs).

◁ The author is trying to discourage a key deer that is begging for food. Several key deer appeared as soon as he started eating his breakfast along a road on Big Pine Key.

People have speculated about why these deer are so small. Their small size may have helped them survive on the Florida Keys, because the food supply is so poor there, or it may have reduced their need for fresh water, which is also scarce on the Keys. It seems that large animals tend to become smaller when isolated on islands. This could be because of poor nutrition. In addition, there is a tendency for mammals of a given species to be smaller as they are found closer to the equator. This theory is known as Bergman's Rule. It is based on the idea that near the equator, animals do not need a large body mass to conserve heat.

Key deer were originally described as a separate species, but there has been considerable dispute about their status. Some authorities still treat them as a full species. However, most authorities now consider them to be a subspecies. Some mammalogists don't believe that they are sufficiently different to even rate that distinction. They are not much different from the mainland white-tailed deer except in size and they are not much smaller than some of the Everglades deer.

Bison

BISON
(*Bison bison*)

Bison are the heaviest native land mammal on the North American continent, 6 feet tall at the hump and weighing 1500 to 2000 pounds.

In spite of their size, they are quick and nimble. They can be very dangerous because of their large size. They should not be closely approached, even though they may look like docile cows. A bison can kill a grizzly bear with its charge. There are more deaths in Yellowstone National Park due to gorings by bison than from bear attacks.

Bison were found throughout all North America at one time, including Florida. They ranged from Mexico to Alaska and from the Atlantic to the Pacific, although they were far more numerous on the Plains than anywhere else. Bison were present in northern Florida until around 1800, and small herds ranged as far south as Payne's Prairie.

In their day, bison were America's most abundant grazing animals. They were a major factor in the ecology of the grasslands over which they roamed, playing a role which to this day is not very well understood.

Bison were the major food source of the Plains Indians, and other Indians traded for them. The meat was dried into jerky, the bison chips (dried dung) used for fires, the hides for robes and tepees, the bones for needles, horns for containers, and tendons for laces. The destruction of the bison caused hardship for the American Indians whose lives were so closely tied to this animal.

White hunters shot bison in great numbers to feed railroad gangs. The last known wild bison east of the Mississippi River was shot in 1832. By 1870 only a fraction of the great herds were left, and between 1870 and 1890, the remaining animals were decimated, slaughtered wantonly for their hides, tongues, and for sport. Bison tongues were considered great delicacies. Whole railroad cars of bison tongues were shipped east and the rest of the carcasses left to rot where they had been shot and had fallen to the ground. The hide hunters and tongue hunters were followed by bone gatherers; the bones were used to make chemicals for refining sugar and were also used for fertilizer.

By 1890 there were less than 1,000 bison in the entire United States. The last herd in the United States at that time, the remnant herd, was in Yellowstone.

△ Male and female bison have different head sizes. The female's head is smaller, with smaller horns.

Today, free-ranging bison can once again be found in Florida in the Payne's Prairie State Preserve just south of Gainesville. They were released into the preserve in 1975, because the state of Florida is trying to restore the original fauna of its natural areas. In early 1993 there were a total of eight bison roaming free within the preserve, but they were hard to see in the tall grasses.

BISON VERSUS BUFFALO

Bison are improperly called "buffalo," but they are not true buffalo. Buffalo properly refers to the water buffalo found in Southeast Asia, and the African cape buffalo. These two animals look similar to the bison, in that they are large, heavy bodied animals with spreading horns, but they are not closely related to the bison. This illustrates the confusion often associated with the use of common names. Famed hunter and showman "Buffalo Bill" Cody probably should have been known as "Bison Bill" Cody.

△ Bison were exterminated in Florida in the 1800s. Now some ranchers are keeping small herds in their pastures as novelties.

THE BIG HERDS

At the time of Columbus, there were an estimated 30 to 75 million bison in North America, mostly between the Rockies and the Mississippi River. The herds stretched for miles, from one horizon to the other, and when they were on the move they could take as much as 5 days to pass by.

Today there are 140,000 bison in North America, mostly in private herds, including some on ranches in Florida. The American Buffalo Association, comprised primarily of people interested in raising bison on ranches, boasts about 1,000 members nationwide. There's also a fairly new animal called a "beefalo," a cross between the bison and a domestic cow or bull, whose tasty meat is lower in fat and cholesterol than regular beef. So far it has not proved to be as popular with the meat-eating public as had been hoped, however. The meat does not have as much marbling as people expect, and many people don't like the idea of eating bison.

FLORIDA'S HABITATS: LOST AND GONE FOREVER?

Of all the various reasons given for the decline of most mammals in Florida, and the disappearance or near disappearance of many, loss of habitat is the most frequently cited and the most serious.

Florida contains perhaps 20 different major habitats or ecological communities, each containing certain species of plants and animals and characterized by specific types of soil, climate, moisture conditions, and certain frequencies of fire. Florida's habitats vary greatly, ranging from very dry scrub to underwater grass flats, including pine flatwoods, hardwood forests (called hammocks), freshwater marshes and swamps, mangrove swamps, beach dune systems, and grassy prairies. In addition, Florida has habitats not found elsewhere in the United States such as coral reefs and tropical hardwood hammocks.

Animals depend on these habitats for food, water, shelter, and cover from predators. No animal is found in all habitats. Many animals only do well in one habitat or a particular few. As the habitats disappear or are damaged, the animals that depend on them usually disappear too.

Unfortunately, many of Florida's best wildlife habitats have disappeared, or are disappearing, at an alarming, almost unbelievable rate. Development is probably the major cause of the destruction of habitat, but agriculture, including forestry, citrus, and cattle ranching, has also contributed greatly.

Some habitats that were once widespread and extensive are now nearly completely gone. Longleaf pine flatwoods, once the most common type of forest in Florida, were home to many endangered or declining species, including Sherman's fox squirrel and the red-cockaded woodpecker. In just 50 years, however, longleaf pine forests have declined from nearly 8 million acres to less than one million acres and have mostly disappeared from the peninsula.

Marshes, home to many animals including 8 endangered or threatened species, 3 of them mammals, declined from 7 million acres to 3 million acres. Mangroves have been similarly decimated in some parts of coastal Florida, as has most of the scrub on the Lake Wales Ridge in Central Florida and the tropical hardwood hammocks of the Florida Keys. No wonder the animals are disappearing too.

To make matters worse, much of what remains is highly fragmented. Many animals require large areas of a certain kind for breeding and food, but many habitats that were once extensive have been broken into numerous tiny pieces. Consequently, many conservationists and ecologists believe that one of the best things we can do to help save Florida's endangered wildlife is to connect the habitats that remain with corridors, wide strips of native vegetation through which animals can travel safely from one natural area to another. In this way, we can perhaps provide some animals with the space they require.

Wild Hog

WILD HOG
(Sus scrofa)

Wild hogs are pigs of mostly domestic origin living in a wild state. Popular Florida "cracker" nicknames are "razorback," referring to the prominent backbone on thin animals and the long, coarse hairs on their back which stand erect when the "razorback" is agitated, and "piney woods rooter," a reference to their habit of rooting in the soil. Other common names include wild boar, wild pig, feral pig, feral hog, and feral swine.

Pigs were brought to the West Indies by Columbus in 1493, and the Spanish explorer DeSoto brought them to Florida in 1539 to provide food for his troops. Domestic pigs were commonly kept on farms for lard and cured meat in the past, and many hogs were allowed to run wild, to be trapped or hunted later for food. European wild boars, extirpated in Europe, except in hunting preserves, were also brought here in the past several centuries for hunting purposes.

The wild hogs found throughout Florida today are a mixture of Spanish wild boars, European hunting stock, Russian boars, and the domestic hogs from farms in Florida that were released to roam free. (Florida had "open ranges" until 1952.) Their predominant color is black, although brown hogs and spotted hogs are also common.

Wild hogs usually roam in groups of several females with their young. The boars (males) are generally solitary except when associated with breeding groups, but the females and young hogs are highly social. Hogs are very adaptable and found in a number of different habitats, but they prefer wooded areas close to water. They are not territorial.

Wild hogs are opportunistic feeders. They eat nearly anything, including roots, tubers, grasses, small animals, and carrion. They are sometimes even cannibalistic. Mast, which consists of fallen acorns and nuts, is a favorite food. They feed mostly at night, especially in summer when it is hot during the day.

If their population is not kept under control, wild hogs often devastate natural habitats. They consume such large amounts of food that they may reduce the food supply available to other animals, such as deer, rabbits, squirrels, and turkey.

Even more damage is caused by their rooting, which is their natural feeding behavior. They badly disrupt native veg-

△ Because they do not have sweat glands, hogs regulate their body temperatures by lying in water or mud, which is why they are often found around rivers in woods and lowlands. Wild hogs may die from becoming overheated. Without plentiful water, they cannot live in a hot climate.

etation, making an area look like it has been plowed. They also cause damage to timber plantations and crops. For many years wild hogs were trapped and relocated in Myakka River State Park. Their digging has done a lot of damage to low vegetation there. For this reason, in recent years the objective has been to remove the hogs from the park.

Wild hogs are a reservoir of serious diseases. They carry pseudorabies, a disease that can be transmitted and fatal to panthers, as well as diseases transmissible to other mammals, including man and livestock. Swine brucellosis can be fatal to humans, so their mucous and blood should be avoided and gloves worn when wild hogs are cleaned. They also carry many parasites, including trichinosis, which is why pork must be cooked properly. (Now that commercial hogs are raised in a much cleaner fashion, however, and no longer fed garbage, trichinosis is mostly a disease of the past.)

Wild hogs breed year round. The females have one or two litters per year, with 5 to 12 piglets in a litter. Infant mortality is relatively low, although the baby pigs sometimes fall prey to hawks, owls, and eagles. In South Florida, panthers prey upon adult wild hogs, and bobcats prey upon young wild hogs

△ The hair on the back of a wild hog bristles if the animal is disturbed.

throughout the state.

Their high reproductive rate and their intelligence help make wild hogs the most successful naturalized large mammal in the United States. (A naturalized species is one that is not native but reproduces and survives in the wild.)

△ A pig "singing" contest provides entertainment at the Iowa State Fair.

HOG INTELLIGENCE

Hogs are reputed to be very intelligent because they can perform feats such as opening gates, and it is known that they have a good memory. Their keen senses, awareness of their environment, and resourcefulness are attributes useful for finding food and surviving in the wild. These same attributes could be associated with curiosity, learning ability, and problem solving, traits that contribute to the hog's reputation as an intelligent animal. But hog intelligence has not yet been subjected to controlled scientific testing. So statements such as "hogs are smarter than dogs" may or may not be true.

HATRED OF PIGS AND THE EATING OF PORK

While adding a little pork fat to everything may be a standard part of southern cooking, eating the flesh of pigs is considered taboo in many parts of the world.

Both Judaism and Islam forbid the eating of pork and the more conservative followers of these religions take the doctrine very, very seriously. In countries where Jews or Moslems live side-by-side with members of other religions, conflicts arise. This is especially true where the other people are Chinese, because pork is such an important part of the Chinese diet.

Both Jews and Moslems depend on government departments to enforce standards for foods, one of which is that it should not contain any trace of pork. Such certified foods are labeled halal (for Moslems) and kosher (for Jews).

In countries of Asia with Moslem populations, rumors sometimes start that certain foods which are supposed to be halal actually contain pork, and violent riots have sometimes occurred as a result.

But hatred of pigs goes well beyond the fear that disease might result from eating pork (which in times past was a very reasonable fear). In 1993 there were riots among Moslems in China because a book publisher printed a drawing which showed a pig in the same scene with a Moslem.

TUSKS AND DOGS – THE HUNTING OF PIGS

Wild hogs are not aggressive and generally run away if approached in the woods. They can be very vicious when cornered, however. A 5-foot boar can weigh as much as 400 pounds, with sharp, 6-inch long tusks (although most hogs are in the 200 pound range). Although sometimes used for defense, the tusks are primarily used for grubbing in the ground.

Wild hogs are hunted with a pack of dogs, usually pit bulls, with their ears trimmed off so the boar can't get hold of them. The dogs will pick up the scent, chase the pig and grab it by the ears or the neck, and ride it until the hog is exhausted. The dogs lock their jaws and hold on. The hog is then shot or tied up by its hind legs. Although the hog has, by then, been badly torn up by the dogs, this is considered great sport by some hunters. Many dogs are also badly injured in this type of hunt.

If captured alive, the hogs are fattened before slaughter. Wild hogs are sometimes castrated and released, so that when recaptured later their meat will not have as strong a taste. Such individuals are called "bar" hogs.

Hunting is the primary cause of death for wild hogs in Florida. With the landowner's permission, wild hogs can be shot year round on private property, where by law they are considered domestic livestock and can be treated like any other domestic animal. In the State's wildlife management areas they are considered game animals, and there they may only be hunted in season with a license. There are estimated to be 500,000 wild hogs in Florida, more than in any other state, and the annual kill is 50,000 or more.

△ The dangerous two-inch teeth of the wild hog are razor sharp and can disembowel a hunting dog or other animal with a single toss of the head. Wild hogs are not normally aggressive, but they may charge and defend themselves if attacked or cornered.

Dolphin

BOTTLE-NOSED DOLPHIN
(Tursiops truncatus)

Dolphins are sea mammals. As mammals, they share certain characteristics with all other mammals. They breathe air and for this reason must come to the surface continually. Their young are born alive and suckle milk the same as other mammals, except the external dolphin teats are located within two mammary slits. Dolphins have hair on the front of their heads, although their hair is not like that of humans. It is extremely sparse and barely noticeable.

The name dolphin comes from the Greek word "delphys" meaning womb, an origin which shows reverence for the life-giving sea. Greek gods such as Apollo sometimes took the form of dolphins. The famous Temple of Delphi and the ancient Oracle of Delphi honor Apollo in his dolphin form. Images of dolphins on coins and jewelry were often used to represent safe journeys and good luck. The fish symbol which was used long ago to mark the secret meeting places of persecuted Christians may have been derived from the reli-

gious symbolism of the dolphin.

The bottle-nosed dolphin is found in temperate waters around the world, in both the northern and southern hemisphere. It is usually seen close to shore, where its prey is found, and seldom seen in the open ocean. In Florida it has a range similar to that of the striped mullet, its main source of food.

Bottle-nosed dolphins have an average length of 9 feet and weigh about 400 pounds. Individual dolphins can be identified by the shape of their dorsal fins and

COUNTERSHADING

Dolphins are dark above and light colored below. A fish looking up at a dolphin is less likely to spot the predator, because the light-colored belly of the dolphin seems to blend with the sky. Similarly, a fish swimming above a dolphin sees its dark back which blends with the water color. Countershading is widespread among many animals including fish, reptiles, birds, and most mammals.

markings. At birth they are about 3 feet long and 25 pounds in weight. They live as long as 30 to 50 years in the wild. Their age can be determined by examining their teeth, which form growth rings much like trees.

Dolphins have a highly streamlined body shape. The male genitals are stored inside the dolphin's body, and dolphins have no external ears. This reduces drag in the water. The dolphin's skin also secretes oils which further speed and smooth the flow of water over the body.

The birth of a baby dolphin is often assisted by the other dolphins in the group. They push the newborn dolphin to the surface for its first breath. Newborn dolphins can swim immediately. They are relatively precocious, compared to humans which stay with their parents longer than any other mammal.

It is not known whether the male plays any significant role in raising the young. The major bond in dolphin society is between the mother and the calf. Although calves can swim immediately after birth, they nurse for over one and a half years and may not even sample fish for the first six months. This in part explains the strong bond between the mother and baby, a bond which lasts from several years to as long as ten years.

Dolphins eat many kinds of fish and squid, consuming over 15 pounds per day. They wait

△ Feeding behavior: dolphins knock a fish into the air with their beak, stunning it, and then pick it up and swallow it.

DOLPHIN COURTSHIP

Florida fishermen report often seeing dolphins mating in groups of three: a female with two males, one male swimming on each side of the female. Since the pair that is mating roll onto their sides, the extra male may help by steadying the female in this awkward position. Dolphins may be the only mammals other than man whose sexual activity is not limited to a certain season but continues virtually year-round.

Dolphins are promiscuous and have an extremely active and unusual sex life. Males often leave their territories and travel long distances to mate with females in other areas. Young male dolphins have been observed copulating with their mothers not long after birth.

Dolphins engage in a complicated courtship ritual which includes caressing, beating their tails against the water, and leaping into the air. Copulation is usually belly to belly under water. The pair sometimes must take a break to go to the surface to breathe.

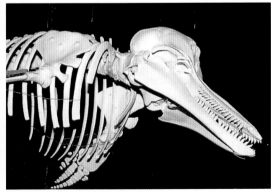

△ Note the conical shape of the dolphin's teeth. This shape allows the dolphin to get a powerful grip on its prey.

in the passes between Florida's barrier islands while the tide ebbs or flows to capture fish passing through. They also capture fish by trapping them against the shore or corralling them in a cooperative effort with other dolphins. The group may surround a school of fish and chase them up onto the shore. In this type of hunt, dolphins sometimes roll onto the land to grab the fish and then roll back into the water. In the water, dolphins sometimes use their tails to injure or stun fish prior to swallowing them.

It is estimated that there are about 100 dolphins in the Sarasota area and nearly 300 in the Sanibel-Captiva area. Mullet is their primary food in Florida. Dolphins will not take baited hooks, probably because they are too intelligent. It is possible that they may even be able to recognize a metal hook through their echolocation.

Dolphins like to follow shrimp trawlers and other fishing vessels that throw fish overboard, and they have learned to take fish off hooks or take advantage of the disturbance caused by netting to catch fish. They have also learned to remove fish from gill nets, sometimes angering fishermen so much that they are willing to risk prosecution to shoot the dolphins. Dolphins attracted to fishing nets sometimes get tangled in the nets themselves.

Dolphins are social animals and are rarely seen alone. They live and travel in small groups, usually 10 or less, and have a complex social order which is essential to their hunting and reproduction.

A group of dolphins is called a pod. In Florida the pods are usually one of three types: females with young, males, or older males. The group does not always stay together. Some members may split off for a while and return to the group later, especially when food is plentiful and hunting as a group is more rewarding. The typical home range of the bottle-nosed dolphin in Florida is 14 square miles.

▷ Television's "Flipper" was a bottle-nosed dolphin, the same as the ones commonly seen in Florida

△ Dolphins seem to like being around people and often swim around boats. They like to ride off the bow of a boat, gliding along with a boost from the bow wave. They can swim up to 20 or 25 mph.

DANGERS TO DOLPHINS

Tuna fishing has been responsible for the death of large numbers of dolphins. Until the 1980s, tens of thousands of dolphins (usually spotted dolphins or spinner dolphins) were killed annually by the United States tuna industry during the taking of red or dark tuna in giant purse nets. In the taking of light tuna (yellowfin tuna), however, few dolphins were killed because different techniques were used.

Now, because of legislation, strict enforcement, and pressure from consumer boycotts, the United States tuna industry has changed. Today most "incidental" dolphin deaths, the unintentional killing of dolphins while fishing for other seafood, is due to the activities of foreign tuna boats.

There are countries like Chile that kill thousands of dolphins in order to use their flesh for bait, while still other countries, namely Japan, allow open season on dolphins by fishermen who feel dolphins are competitors. Pollution of the seas poses another serious threat to dolphins.

The federal Marine Mammal Protection Act prohibits the capture or harassment of dolphins and whales and prohibits the removal of dead dolphins from the beach. (This aids enforcement; a person cannot claim that a dead dolphin in his possession washed up on the beach as opposed to being slaughtered in the water.)

Dolphins are subject to parasites and disease, and sick animals sometimes beach themselves for reasons still not known. In 1987, a warm-water bacterium may have been responsible for the death of from 20 to 50 percent of Atlantic bottle-nosed dolphins. The National Marine Fisheries Service has declared the coastal populations of dolphins depleted and are investigating the current population trends.

DO DOLPHINS REALLY SAVE DROWNING SWIMMERS?

There are reports of dolphins helping swimmers including one incident on the Florida coast in 1943. A woman caught in an undertow was given a tremendous shove toward shore, presumably by a dolphin which was seen nearby. It is not known whether such behavior is purposeful help, play behavior, or the result of the instincts which lead dolphin mothers to push their young to the surface and adult dolphins to assist injured companions

DOLPHINS IN CAPTIVITY

Dolphins probably live longer in captivity than in the wild. Dolphins born in captivity can be released and will survive in the wild. Experience has shown that most dolphins that have lived in captivity in coastal pens, if intentionally or accidentally released, tend to return to the place where they had been enclosed. It is very difficult to rehabilitate dolphins if they become ill in captivity or are found sick in the wild.

The taking of dolphins is strictly regulated by the federal government. Yet the capturing of these intelligent creatures for use in animal shows has been very controversial. There is a high death rate when dolphins are captured because nets are used and the dolphins sometimes drown in the nets. There have been incidents in Charlotte Harbor and other places in Florida in which animal rights activists disrupted the legal, permitted capture of dolphins by chasing the dolphins out of the area.

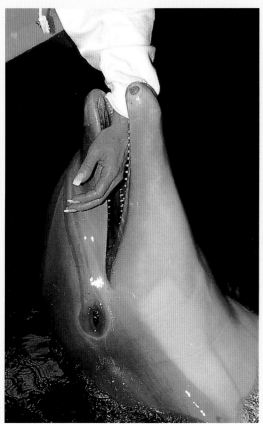

SELLING DOLPHINS

There is a market for live dolphins, and they are worth thousands of dollars each. Nearly 50 per year were removed from the wild in the United States in the 1970s, but that's a very small number in relation to their total numbers.

Dolphins are very popular in tourist attractions, but keeping dolphins in captivity is controversial. Some people feel that it is morally wrong to capture and confine such intelligent creatures for profit. However, these attractions may benefit dolphins by increasing public interest and support for conservation programs.

DOLPHIN SONAR

Dolphins practice echolocation under water in a manner similar to bats in the air. They send out sounds of various frequencies and use the echoes to track prey, detect obstacles, and for other purposes. A dolphin's brain is very large in proportion to its body (similar to that of a human). This may be due to the complex processing required in echolocation.

Dolphins can produce and distinguish up to 700 sounds per second. This is 20 times more sounds than a human is able to distinguish. The "melon," the bulging forehead of the dolphin, is filled with a waxy substance which may help direct the clicks, whistles, and squeaking sounds that dolphins make for echolocation.

One secret of echolocation is that a dolphin's earbones are not in direct contact with its skull. This allows it to pinpoint the direction of sound waves more accurately by clearly separating the outgoing and incoming signals.

To what extent dolphin sounds are used for communication rather than sonar is not yet fully known. Some dolphins are capable of producing extremely loud sounds underwater which may be used to stun their prey.

SWIMMING WITH DOLPHINS

Dolphins seem to like the presence of people and interact well with them. A research facility in the Florida Keys has used this trait to develop a program to help children with learning disabilities. Researchers had the idea that many children with mental disabilities were capable of learning but could not pay attention long enough to do so.

At the Dolphin Research Center, children whose problems ranged from Down's syndrome to retardation and mild autism were encouraged to concentrate their minds by the presence of dolphins. Sitting on the dock with a dolphin swimming nearby, the child was asked to do a task such as saying a word, identifying a picture, or picking up an object. If the child succeeded, he or she was rewarded by being allowed to feed, touch, or swim with the dolphins. On alternate weeks the same sessions were conducted in a classroom, where the rewards were a hug, a kiss, or verbal praise. The children responded from two to ten times better in the presence of the dolphins, and at no time did the classroom results ever exceed the results obtained with the help of the dolphins in holding the attention of the children. Parents remarked that they had never seen their children show so much interest in anything.

Now that research has shown this new learning procedure to be effective, the Dolphin Research Center is establishing therapy programs to help more disabled children. DRC is a privately owned, non-profit organization which sponsors other programs such as dolphin-human interaction seminars.

DOLPHIN INTELLIGENCE

Dolphins are easy to train, but whether their intelligence approaches the intelligence of human beings is not known. The huge size of a dolphin's brain, the sophistication of its sonar, its social organization, its use of sounds to communicate, and even its basic friendliness and curiosity have all led to speculation about its intelligence. However, predictions in the past few decades about human communication with dolphins and other species have not yet come to pass.

The current research on dolphin intelligence is still inconclusive, especially when it goes beyond their ability to survive in the wild. The comparison of dolphin intelligence to human intelligence is difficult, and perhaps meaningless, because many of their brain functions and life styles are so different. How is it possible to compare the awesome brain power required for echolocation, for example, with the intelligent acts of humans or chimps?

DOLPHINS, PORPOISES, AND WHALES

Dolphins and porpoises are both air-breathing sea mammals, and their names are sometimes used interchangeably. Both have echolocation and both use blowholes for breathing, but they differ in other ways. Porpoises have rounded heads; they lack the "beak" of the dolphin (the extension of the head below the forehead, sometimes described as a long snout). The dorsal fin on a porpoise's back is triangular in shape, while that of a dolphin is larger than that of a porpoise and very concave on its trailing edge. Porpoises have leaf-shaped teeth while dolphins have larger, conical teeth.

To further confuse matters, there is a common fish also called dolphin, or mahi mahi, which is a popular dish in many California and Hawaiian restaurants.

Dolphins, porpoises, and whales are all related and belong to the order Cetacea. The Cetacea are then divided into two subgroups, the toothed whales and the baleen whales. Baleen whales have baleen plates through which they strain thousands of small organisms, such as plankton and small fish, from the sea water. Dolphins, along with porpoises, sperm whales, and beaked whales, belong to the group of toothed whales.

DOLPHINS AND SHARKS

Some people believe that the presence of dolphins guarantees that the water is free of sharks and therefore safe for humans. This is a myth. Sharks and dolphins sometimes travel together, although each has been known to attack the other.

SLEEPING UNDER WATER

Dolphins sleep while lolling near the surface. Part of a dolphin's brain must remain functional during sleep so it can surface to breathe. Dolphins need less sleep than most mammals, perhaps because they can rest their muscles during waking periods by floating.

SPOTTED DOLPHINS
(Stella frontalis and Stenella attenuata)

Spotted dolphins are similar in appearance to bottle-nosed dolphins but can be distinguished by their numerous light-colored spots. They are generally found in deeper water than bottle-nosed dolphins, usually more than five miles offshore rather than in coastal habitats. There are two species of spotted dolphins in Florida waters. They are found on both the Atlantic and Gulf coasts.

DOLPHINS AND TUNA FISHING

Dolphins and tuna are both found in the same area and both feed on the same bait fish. Fishermen sometimes look for dolphins in order to find tuna, since dolphins must surface and are highly visible. In the past, many dolphins were killed when they became entangled in the nets set for tuna and drowned when they could not surface to breathe. Recent legislation has required fishermen to use nets that have special openings allowing the dolphins to escape. Most of the tuna fishing takes place in the tropical East Pacific off the coast of Peru. The dolphins involved are mostly spinner and spotted dolphins.

SPINNER DOLPHIN
(Stenella longirostris)

The common name is derived from the spinner dolphin's habit of leaping out of the water and spinning on its long axis, sometimes making two or more rotations each leap. Spinner dolphins, as well as spotted dolphins, often ride the bow waves of boats for long distances.

◁ The spinner dolphin is distinguished from the bottle-nosed dolphin and the spotted dolphins by its long snout, slender body, and distinctive color pattern, with a black tipped snout, gray back, tan sides, and white belly.

OTHER DOLPHINS AND WHALES IN FLORIDA

Most of the marine mammals found in the Atlantic Ocean have been observed in Florida coastal waters including more than 25 species of dolphins and whales, although many of these are known from only a single or a few individuals found dead on the beach.

Two large baleen whales which are encountered in Florida waters fairly frequently are the right whale and the humpback whale. Much of the western Atlantic population of right whales apparently winters just offshore along the east coast of Florida and Georgia. Right whales are often observed by fishermen and naturalists off the east coast from Fernandina Beach south to Cape Canaveral, a region that also appears to be their winter calving grounds where the females give birth. Humpback whales regularly occur off the Atlantic coast of Florida in the fall and spring as they migrate between their summer feeding

grounds off eastern Canada and Cape Cod and their winter calving grounds in the southern Bahamas.

Among the more than 20 species of toothed whales found in Florida waters are three species of sperm whales, four species of beaked whales, and about 14 kinds of dolphins. With the exception of the Atlantic bottle-nosed dolphin and several other species regularly seen in captivity, such as the killer whale, most people will never see live individuals of these species because they occur in deep waters far offshore. The bottle-nosed dolphin is by far the most common dolphin in Florida and is the only cetacean regularly observed in the state's shallow coastal waters and estuaries. The pygmy sperm whale is probably the second most common cetacean in Florida based on the number of dead stranded individuals found on beaches. Unfortunately these

small sperm whales are very rarely observed alive. Every ten years or so a large group or pod of pilot whales strands on one of Florida's beaches, generally causing quite a stir among local residents and the media. More than 100 pilot whales beached themselves on the Atlantic coast near Mayport in northeastern Florida in the late 1970s. As is often the case in mass strandings of whales, most of the animals perished despite the intense efforts of many whale-lovers.

In fact, much of what is known about Florida's rarer dolphins and whales has been discovered through the study of dead, stranded animals. However, if a nonprofessional encounters a stranded sea mammal on a beach, dead or alive, the Florida Marine Patrol should be called, because it is against the law for private individuals to handle any species of marine mammal.

Manatee

WEST INDIAN MANATEE
(*Trichechus manatus*)

The name "manatee" probably comes from a Carib Indian word meaning "breast," because the manatee is a sea creature that nurses its young. (All mammals nurse their young.) Manatees are also called sea cows, a reference to their large size and their slow grazing on vegetation. The scientific name *manatus* means "having hands," because the manatee is known for its dexterous use of its flippers. The West Indian manatee was once also called the nail manatee, because it has fingernails on its front flippers (and some of the other manatee species do not). These heavy nails are used to dig into the bottom of streams and tear up roots.

Manatees belong to the order Sirenia, named for the sirens of Greek mythology whose singing, according to legend, lured sailors to their death on rocky reefs. The four species in this group are all tropical or subtropical: the dugong (Northern Australia and Indian Ocean); West African manatee; Amazonian manatee (Amazon basin); and the species found in Florida and the Caribbean, the West Indian manatee. Sirenians are the only aquatic mammals that are primarily vegetarian. Female manatees are called cows, males, bulls, and the young, calves.

Manatees are not predators themselves, and there are no animals that prey on them except for man and possibly sharks. They reach 13 feet or more in length and weigh around 1,200 pounds, although some may reach a weight of 3,500 pounds or even more. They eat over 60 species of plants and forage on seagrass beds in bays, estuaries, and coastal rivers. It is this dependence on vegetation near the shore that makes manatees so vulnerable to human-caused death.

Manatees ingest snails and other small animals found on and among the sea grasses on which they feed. The shells of these creatures provide calcium and phospho-

△ Manatees do not seem to mind contact with humans. Diving with manatees is allowed in Crystal River, with some restrictions to protect the animals against harassment.

rus which the manatees require. There are also reports of manatees occasionally feeding on fish. This deviation from their vegetarian diet may be an important source of protein. In captivity, manatees need supplemental minerals to remain healthy.

THE MERMAID MYTH

The manatee (or, more likely, its close relative, the Indo-Pacific dugong) is famed as the real-life inspiration for the mermaid myth. Sailors who had been at sea too long supposedly spotted the creatures and let their imaginations run wild (or were inspired to deliberately invent the yarn).

But the affection and fascination many people feel for manatees really needs no mythology. These gentle animals deserve understanding and protection. New legislation, if approved, will control boat speeds and regulate diving for the benefit of manatees. Most manatee deaths in Florida today are the result of collisions with boats. Although manatees also face problems such as siltation killing the sea grass that they eat, reducing the hazard of boats is the one factor that should be easiest to control.

Manatees' nostrils have special valves to keep water out when they are submerged. Their lungs and diaphragm run lengthwise along the body, unlike other mammals, in which they run crosswise. This supposedly provides balance in the water. The many muscles surrounding the lungs allow manatees to expel air more rapidly than other animals, thus making it possible for them to submerge quickly. They can remain submerged for up to 15 minutes but generally don't stay down that long. The minimal amount of body hair (except for whiskers) and the lack of hind limbs and external ears all help reduce friction when the manatee glides through the water. The flattened tail provides propulsion and also serves as a rudder.

Although manatees have no external ears, they have internal ears and can hear very well. In fact, mother and calf use sound to communicate with each other. Their conspicuous facial whiskers and flippers also provide tactile feedback. They touch each other often. Manatees also seem to have good eyesight, because they are good at discriminating different shapes, sizes, and colors. They are quite intelligent, with a good attention span, good learning ability, and good retention.

The total population of manatees in Florida is small. There may be as many as 2,000 or fewer than 1,000, depending on the source, and their numbers are probably declining slowly. They live well over 30 years in captivity, but no one knows what age they might attain in the wild. Their natural life span is probably as much as 60 to 70 years.

△ Manatees have nostrils that can close to keep out water. Note that the manatee on the right has its nostrils open and the one on the left has its nostrils closed.

Manatee populations are now considered stable, but a small increase in manatee mortality could spell disaster over a period of time. Among the reasons the manatee population in Florida is not growing (besides suffering a lot of deaths from human causes), is that manatees are very slow at reproducing. Before a female manatee can have her first calf, she must be at least four to six years old. She generally has only one calf at a time (although a few cases of twins have been recorded) and usually does not have another for about two to five years.

◁ These manatees are cleaning the algae from each others' backs. Note the areas already cleaned. Their large and very moveable upper lips, aided by their dexterous flippers, are not only suitable for cleaning algae. They also allow a manatee to pull large amounts of vegetation into its mouth. The prehensile lips actually extend so they can gather more food, with the stiff facial bristles acting as little rakes.

Manatees are considered semi-social animals. The basic social bond is between mother and calf. Small groups of animals sometimes travel together, but these are not permanent groupings. Large numbers may congregate in warm waters during winter months, and during this time there are many social interactions like cavorting, nuzzling, and a lot of vocalizing. However, manatees have no leaders, they are not territorial, and there is no aggression other than pushing and shoving among males for access to females. Manatees of all ages have been observed at play.

West Indian manatees range from Florida to Mexico and Central America and as far south as Brazil. They are found in fresh, brackish, or marine water, clear or muddy, and they seem to prefer depths of three to nine feet. On the west coast of Florida, they may be found as far north as the Suwannee River in summer and the Withlacoochee River in winter. On the east coast, manatees rarely go farther north than North Carolina in warm weather. They are also found inland in Lake Okeechobee and the upper St. Johns River. Manatees do not migrate in the usual sense, but there is a general movement southward during winter months because that is where warmer water can be found.

MOVING TEETH

Manatees spend many hours a day feeding. Some of the larger animals may consume hundreds of pounds of vegetation per day. This great amount of food, and its coarseness, causes the manatees' teeth to be worn down. The large amount of sand taken in with the vegetation also wears the teeth. Replacement teeth move up from the rear of the mouth as the front teeth are worn down and fall out. The tooth row moves forward as new teeth erupt in the back. (Elephants and kangaroos replace their teeth in a similar manner and for similar reasons.)

DANGER TO MANATEES

Manatees were heavily exploited in the 19th and early 20th century, their hides made into leather, their bones worked like ivory, and their delectable meat eaten. Manatee meat is described as delicious, often compared to fine beef. Their bones have also been found in pre-Columbian villages, evidence that they have been hunted for food for thousands of years.

Efforts to protect manatees began many years ago. Florida was declared a manatee sanctuary by the British in the 18th century. Manatees have been protected by Florida laws since 1893 and federal laws since 1972, but poaching continued into the 1980s.

Today, manatees are protected from capture or harassment by the Endangered Species Act and the Marine Mammal Protection Act. Violators may be punished with fines of up to $20,000 and imprisonment up to one year. Over 20 areas in Florida are regulated as official manatee sanctuaries.

Hunting and cold winters were the principal causes of death in the past, but 75% of manatee deaths in Florida today are caused by boats and barges. Manatees can swim as fast as 15 mph for short distances but usually cruise at about two to six miles per hour. This slowness makes them especially vulnerable to boats.

Almost all manatees in Florida are deeply scarred from contact with boat propellers. Over 900 individuals have been catalogued by their scars. Now there are Manatee Zones posted to slow boats in areas where manatees gather.

The next largest cause of manatee deaths today is pneumonia and possibly other bronchial illnesses caused by cold weather. Deaths have also been associated with red tide. In 1990, a record year, 201 manatee deaths were recorded in Florida. Infant mortality is a special concern because of the manatee's low reproductive rate.

As with most threatened or endangered mammals, however, loss of habitat is probably the most serious long-term threat to their continued survival in Florida. There has been considerable loss of the grass flats where manatees feed.

△ The marks on the back of this manatee are scars from its encounters with speedboats. Although manatees can move quickly when necessary, it is not always possible for them to avoid speeding boats. It is especially dangerous for them now because of the dramatic increase in pleasure craft. Where manatees gather, the state of Florida has posted speed limits for boaters. A scientific study is now underway to determine how well manatees can hear boats approaching.

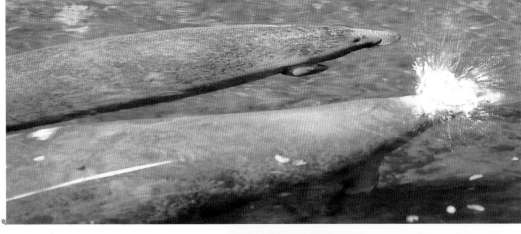

△ Manatees are large aquatic mammals which must surface frequently to breathe. In the photo above, one of the manatees is exhaling at the surface, making a big splash.

◁ Female manatee nursing its calf. The manatee's nipple is located behind its front flipper. Calves nurse underwater, their heads buried in the "armpit" underneath the mother's front flipper. Calves remain with their mothers up to two years. Manatee calves weigh 60 to 80 pounds at birth and start nibbling on plants about a month after they are born. Females have been known to adopt and nurse orphaned calves.

A female in heat will usually be accompanied by a number of males. Large herds form as more and more males follow a female, for as long as a month, until she is ready to breed. Once ready to mate, the female will usually mate with more than one male.

△ This manatee has a radio transmitter attached to its tail which will be used for tracking. Transmissions are monitored through a satellite. The tether allows the transmitter to float at the surface for better transmission. If the manatee tangles the tether in weeds, it will come off. It is designed to come off eventually through corrosion of the harness. Radios allow researchers to track the manatees' movements and monitor water temperatures.

◁ The large, flat manatee tail is adapted to provide propulsion, to move the animal on its journeys along the coasts and through the inland waterways. The up and down motion of the tail is similar to that of a dolphin tail, but the shape is quite different,

SURVIVING THE COLD WEATHER

Manatees lack a thick layer of insulating fat. In addition, their metabolism is so low that they cannot generate a lot of body heat. For these reasons they require minimum water temperatures of about 68 degrees and cannot tolerate water that is below 61 degrees. In colder water they often die. The reasons are not clear. It is thought that the cold water causes them to suffer from pneumonia. In 1989, 46 manatees were found dead following a 3-day freeze.

When the air temperature gets down to about 50 degrees, manatees gather in groups called pods and head for warm water sites. In Florida, they seek the warmer water of natural springs where the temperature remains constant all year. These include such well-known manatee gathering spots as Crystal River and Blue Springs.

Manatees have also learned to take advantage of power plants with warm-water discharge, such as the one at Riviera Beach. There are presently about 24 warm water sources in Florida where manatees congregate in winter, in groups of as many as one hundred. This is when they are most often observed. (There

were 287 manatees at Crystal River in the winter of 1990 and 50 to 100 each winter at Blue Springs State Park.) In summer they go out into the coastal waters and are less visible. The coastal waters in summer are warmer than the water in the springs.

△ A group of manatees attempting to get close to the source of warm spring water during a winter cold spell. Manatees have been observed remaining motionless, as still as logs, for many hours.

MANATEE EXHIBITS

The Lowry Park Zoo in Tampa has an excellent new manatee exhibit, and there are also fine exhibits at Sea World near Orlando. Some of the manatee exhibits feature animals that are being rehabilitated from injuries.

Many Floridians are working to help the manatees. In addition to the efforts of state agencies, there are private organizations raising funds and public awareness. Special license plates with a picture of a manatee are available for an additional fee with the extra money earmarked for conservation efforts.

▷ The skin of the manatee is rough to the touch, as the young lady in this photo is learning for herself.

USE OF MANATEES FOR WEED CONTROL

Since large manatees can consume hundreds of pounds of vegetation daily, it seemed logical that they might be superior to toxic poisons in controlling aquatic weeds, such as the hyacinths and hydrilla that clog many Florida waterways. An extra benefit of reducing the weeds would be the elimination of the mosquitos that breed among the weeds. In 1966 an experiment tested the effectiveness of using manatees for weed control. A number of manatees were captured and placed in a canal from which they could not escape. Although the manatees did consume enough weeds to keep the canal clear, restricting the movement of the animals proved fatal. Cold weather and poachers killed most of the manatees. In Florida, manatees must take refuge in warm water during cold spells.

Researchers later estimated that the number of manatees required to keep pace with fast-growing weeds in larger waterways would be very large. Considering the slow reproductive rate of manatees and the small number of animals present in Florida, it became obvious that manatees were not capable of coping with the problem. It would take all the manatees in Florida working all summer to consume the existing mass of weeds in just one bay without even making allowance for new growth.

Ferret

FERRET (*Mustela putorius*)

Ferrets are commonly kept as pets. They are actually domesticated European weasels. They are not a wise choice for a pet because they are capable of inflicting severe bites. They have never established a breeding population in Florida, although many escape. Still, there is considerable fear that if this animal became established in the wilds of Florida, many small mammals, birds, and reptiles would be threatened, because ferrets are such voracious hunters.

INTRODUCED SPECIES

Florida has more introduced plants and animals than any other state in the continental United States. At least ten mammal species that were originally absent from Florida have been introduced or recently arrived here and are now surviving in the wild.

Introduced mammals that are now found throughout all or much of Florida include the wild hog (a major game species), black rat and Norway rat, house mouse, ferret, and the nine-banded armadillo, and the nutria.

Those with a narrow distribution include the sambar deer (St. Vincent Island), black-tailed jackrabbit (the eastern edge of the Everglades), red-bellied squirrel (Elliot Key), rhesus monkey (Silver Springs), and possibly the jaguarundi and coati.

Other exotic (non-native) mammals that have been released in Florida include spider monkeys, European rabbit, prairie dog, ring-tail, ocelot, jaguar, and black leopard. Probably none of these reproduce and survive in the wild in Florida

There are two basic problems caused by the introduction of non-native species (which are often defined as those species not found here prior to the first European contact—that is, in the period before Columbus, or pre-Columbian times). If they survive in the wild, they may crowd out native species. In addition, the natural predators that would normally keep their populations in check might be absent here, in which case they may become abundant enough to be health hazards, cause agricultural damage, or compete with native species for resources.

To guard against the establishment of exotic species, Florida law prohibits the release of non-native wildlife. Most exotic animals cannot survive in the wild, so besides the problems they might cause, releasing them is cruel to the animals themselves.

Monkeys

RHESUS MONKEY
(Macaca mulata)

Rhesus monkeys, part of the macaque group, range from Afghanistan to Indochina. They have a nasty disposition, and the males can be aggressive toward humans, especially if they are stared at, because they interpret a stare as a threat. They have been imported in the past primarily because of their great importance as research animals. Many diseases of man also affect monkeys.

There are two colonies of rhesus monkeys in Florida at the present time. One colony is on an island in the lower Keys, but this is not a free-ranging population. These monkeys were established on the island by a pharmaceutical company for the purpose of producing a supply of the animals for research. The monkeys have fouled the water, killed trees, including large numbers of mangroves, and made a big mess of things in general, alarming people on the nearest inhabited islands. The company cares for the colony under federal guidelines and removes individuals as needed for federal and other research projects.

The other colony, at Silver Springs near Ocala, is the only free-ranging rhesus monkey colony and the only wild population in North America. It is believed that the original owner of the Silver Springs attraction, Columbus Carmichael, released two to four monkeys on an island as an exhibit. They immediately swam away and have been in the wild ever since. Another story is that the monkeys escaped during the filming of a Tarzan movie. This is less likely. Although several monkey species were used in the movie, rhesus monkeys were probably not used because of their bad disposition. No state other than Florida has monkeys surviving in the wild.

TROUBLES WITH ONE TROOP

The rhesus monkeys at Silver Springs now number in the hundreds and have divided into a north troop and a south troop. Silver Springs puts out food, feeling responsible for the monkeys' maintenance, and this tends to keep them from wandering too far, although they occasionally go into the neighboring Ocala National Forest.

At various times there have been plans to capture and kill all the rhesus monkeys at Silver Springs because of the threat of diseases. There have been confrontations between the monkeys and humans there. The area is less isolated than it once was, and people occasionally get upset about the monkeys because they fear the monkeys will attack humans or carry diseases contagious to humans. The monkeys are becoming more numerous, and they are big enough and strong enough to be potentially dangerous to people. Recently, a plan to sterilize the monkeys was proposed in the hope of offending fewer people than killing them would.

SQUIRREL MONKEY
(Saimiri sciureus)

Florida has no native primates other than man. However, there are small populations of monkeys in a few areas. Florida's wild squirrel monkeys come from animals that were imported as pets from South America and later escaped. There have been wild populations in Dade County, in Naples near Caribbean Gardens, and also in Polk County near Lake Wales.

There are 5 different species of squirrel monkeys. The one in Florida comes from east of the Andes, in Colombia, northern Peru, and Brazil. In South America, squirrel monkeys are captured for food, bait, and pets. Nevertheless, this is the most abundant and least threatened primate in South America.

These monkeys are social animals and always travel in troops of family units. They spend all their time in trees. They don't seem to bother people.

In the past, squirrel monkeys were imported into the United States in great numbers for medical research and as pets (173,000 were imported from 1968 through 1972). Federal regulations in 1975 ended the importation of all primates into the United States as pets.

△ The squirrel monkey is a fruit-eater. In this photo it is eating Brazilian pepper berries, an exotic animal eating the fruits of an exotic plant.

JAGUARUNDI
(Felis yagouaroundi)

The jaguarundi, first reported in Florida in 1942, was intentionally introduced at Chiefland and Hillsborough River State Park. It is a thin cat with a small head, short-legs, and a long tail, ranging from reddish-brown to dark gray in color. It may be as much as four feet, eight inches long including its tail.

This wild cat occurs naturally from southern Arizona and southern Texas through Mexico and central America to northern Argentina. Since its introduction in Florida, numerous sightings have been reported in many parts of the state, and a road-killed animal was allegedly found in 1961. However, experts disagree as to whether it has become established here in the wild.

The jaguarundi runs in leaps of more than twenty feet. Its tracks are about the size of a house cat or gray fox. Cat tracks do not have claw marks because their claws are retractable.

COATI
(Nasua narica)

The coati has been sighted off-and-on in various parts of Florida. It is a Latin American version of the raccoon, but with a long snout and a long tail. The name is usually pronounced *coh-wati*.

WILD ANIMALS AS PETS

There are two primary reasons why people should not keep wild animals such as raccoons or skunks as pets in the United States.

First, animals that come from pet shops, often raccoons, may have been trapped in the Everglades or some rural area. They are usually wild raccoons taken at a young age, and they could be harboring rabies. Since the disease might not be evident for a number of months, it is an especially dangerous situation. There is no vaccine currently available for raccoons or other wild animals that offers protection against rabies like the vaccines for cats and dogs.

Second, many people believe it is cruel to capture wild animals and put them into captivity. Raccoons, for example, are wildlife, and many people now feel that they should be treated as such. Wild animals usually don't live up to the expectations of most pet-lovers who would like their animals to be happy in confinement, gentle and responsive to people, and able to adjust to their owners' busy schedules.

Even though young raccoons are cute and cuddly, it is unwise to confine them in a house. Raccoons are very friendly until they reach about a year and a half in age, and then they become very fierce. The males have heated mating battles, and they can tear a house apart trying to get out. In Florida, a permit is required to keep a raccoon. This permit is obtained through the local offices of the Florida Game and Freshwater Fish Commission.

Skunks, too, are often kept as pets. Most skunk owners want their pet de-scented, but to de-scent a skunk is to take away its natural protection. When a de-scented skunk has grown up and is ready to move about on its own, it cannot be released into the wild because it has lost its natural defense.

There are serious problems involving the exotic pet trade that have yet to be resolved. A very large percentage of the animals that are captured in the wild for sale as pets do not survive the ordeal of capture, transport, and life in captivity. This is especially true of animals that are smuggled, because these animals are usually transported under very harsh conditions. This means that many times the number actually sold in pet shops must be taken from wild populations, putting pressure on species that are often already endangered.

People who wish to be involved with wildlife should consider contacting a local Wildlife Rehabilitation Center and working as a volunteer under its training and supervision. This is safer and will benefit wildlife in a far more effective way than keeping orphaned or injured wild animals in a home.

Mexican Red-bellied Squirrel

(Sciurus aureogaster)

This squirrel was imported in 1938 by a local resident who thought that the island on which he was farming needed more mammals. Two pairs were brought from Mexico and released on Elliot Key in what is now Biscayne Bay National Park near Miami. They began breeding, and are now naturalized on Elliot Key and a few other small keys nearby. They swim from one island to another.

Mexican red-bellied squirrels are shy and elusive and very hard to observe. They are usually found in trees, seldom on the ground. They build nests of leaves and sometimes nest in natural cavities. Their population appears to be quite small, but nobody knows for certain. They are very difficult to catch in traps. Trappers reported success on only four nights out of 1,000 in which traps were set.

Mexican red-bellied squirrels, also called Mexican gray squirrels, are similar in color to native gray squirrels, but more variable in color, with a frosty look from their white-tipped hairs. There are two major color phases, a dark, almost black phase, and a gray-brown phase. The gray-brown squirrels have chestnut red bellies from which the species gets its Latin name.

Sambar Deer

(Cervus unicolor niger)

Originally from India, the Sambar deer is found in a wide range of habitats, from mangrove swamps at sea level up to 12,000 feet in the Himalayan foothills. This large Asian deer was introduced to the western world over 2,300 years ago by Alexander the Great when he returned from India. The earliest written description of this animal was provided by Aristotle, so it is also known as Aristotle's deer.

This highly adaptable deer has been introduced and is now established in the wild in Australia, New Zealand, California, Texas, and Florida. It was introduced to Florida early this century by the former owner of St. Vincent Island, now the St. Vincent Island National Wildlife Refuge, off the Florida Panhandle. The herd grew to several hundred but was reduced to about 50 by illegal hunting in the 1940s. Today it numbers about 100.

The dark brown Sambar deer resembles the American elk, to which it is related. It stands nearly 5 feet tall at the shoulders and averages 600 pounds in its home range. Mostly nocturnal, it is comfortable in water and swims readily. Its hoofs are large and splayed, allowing the sambar to support its body weight on marshy ground.

AN UNUSUAL INTRODUCTION OF A NON-NATIVE SPECIES

One of the problems with introducing non-native species is that they often outcompete native species. However, in the introduction of the Mexican red-bellied squirrel, there were no native squirrels on the island for the newcomers to crowd out, and the few predators on the island (birds of prey and snakes) were enough to keep the new arrivals from becoming a problem. The squirrels have, so far, not extended their range beyond a few islands and their numbers remain low because of predation. They have not reached the mainland or Key Biscayne, although Hurricane Andrew in 1992 may have changed the situation. They are being watched and studied by the National Park Service.

These squirrels have done extensive damage to the native thatch palms on Elliot Key. The palm fruits are one of their main foods, but the squirrels also chew the plants themselves, and most of the palms have been damaged.

Although it cannot be said for sure what other harm might come from this introduction, this situation is thus far in sharp contrast to many other species introductions (such as the black and Norway rats, and the house mouse), where more serious problems have resulted. However, the story is not finished and the final chapter cannot be written yet.

HUNTING LAWS IN FLORIDA

There are prescribed seasons for hunting various animals and limits on the numbers that may be taken. A trapping license is required for trapping fur-bearing animals, and Florida has outlawed the leghold trap. The baiting or luring of migratory game birds or black bears is illegal. Dogs may be used in some hunting.

Black-tailed jackrabbit

(Lepus californicus)

Black-tailed jackrabbits normally range through the southwestern part of the United States and into Mexico, but they were introduced into Florida in the 1920s and 30s. Jackrabbits were shipped from western states to Florida to train greyhounds for racing, and some were either intentionally or accidentally released at various places in South Florida.

Black-tailed jackrabbits need open fields where they can see and hear predators and run to escape. The well-mowed, lush, grassy areas adjoining the runways at airports fulfil these requirements. A small population of jackrabbits lives along the runways at the Miami International Airport. These rabbits are much larger than Florida's two native rabbit species, so they are quite conspicuous and easily visible from the jets taxiing along the runways. Passengers often see them leaping or grazing at dawn or dusk.

Jackrabbits lie flat on the ground, where they remain nearly invisible in small depressions called "forms," until a predator or human gets close. Then they suddenly dart away in a zigzag pattern, in leaps of up to twenty feet, as fast as 30 to 35 miles per hour. Every fifth or sixth leap is especially high, providing a better view of the intruder. When at a safe distance, they sit up in typical rabbit fashion, extending and twisting their huge ears, listening and looking for new danger.

In hot weather, jackrabbits use their huge ears for thermal regulation. The numerous blood vessels in the ears disperse heat. This is an adaptation for life in the desert, their natural habitat. They eat day and night, unlike cottontails which are nocturnal feeders. They swim quite well, although they don't take to water readily.

During their mating ritual the males are very rough, sparring with other males with their front feet and running in circles. Like cats, jackrabbits are induced ovulators, meaning that rough copulation induces immediate ovulation in the female. Like many hares, they have a population cycle with peaks in undisturbed populations occurring at about nine year intervals.

Rabbits and hares have become serious pests in many regions where they have been introduced, but jackrabbits have not yet become a serious threat to native animals or agriculture in Florida. The reason is not clear. It would seem that the grasslands of central Florida, with the grassy shoulders and medians of highways as dispersal corridors, would be similar to their habitat at Miami International Airport. One possibility is that Florida is too wet. Jackrabbits thrive in the arid conditions of the western states.

△ Note the long ears. It is thought that these large ears cool the body through a network of blood vessels. Jackrabbits usually live in warm climates.

▽ This black-tailed jackrabbit sits low in a depression to remain out of view.

△ The jackrabbits at Miami International Airport are clearly visible to airline passengers. They seem to prosper on the flat, open land but so far have not extended their range to any large degree. Biologists monitoring these hares wonder why they have not invaded much of Florida. It would seem that the medians and shoulders of highways would be suitable habitat and would provide corridors through which the jackrabbits could expand their range.

RABBITS AND HARES: THE DIFFERENCE

The jackrabbit is actually a hare rather than a rabbit. Hares are usually larger than rabbits and have black-tipped ears. In addition, while young rabbits are born naked, blind, and helpless, hares are born as small miniatures of their parents, fully furred, with their eyes open. Only a few minutes after birth hares are able to run, an adaptation to living in open habitats where there is little cover. The mother drops the young almost anywhere, and they are strong enough to leave the area within twenty-four hours. Such well-developed youngsters are called "precocial." The opposite is "altricial," which means that the young require a long period of nursing. Rabbits are altricial, hares are precocial.

HOW JACKRABBITS WERE ONCE USED TO TRAIN GREYHOUNDS

Jackrabbits were used for many years for training greyhounds because they are faster than other rabbits and they jump high in the air as they run, thus exciting the dogs. The training proceeded in stages. At first, the rabbits were pinched to make them squeal. Jackrabbits make a terrible shrieking sound. (Recordings of this sound are used to attract many mammal predators including coyotes, bobcats, and raccoons.) This drove the greyhounds crazy. The greyhounds were released and allowed to chase and kill the rabbits in enclosed areas. Later, a real rabbit, sometimes live and sometimes dead, was attached to the mechanical rabbit, and the dogs were allowed to chase and catch it. In the final stage, the dogs were willing to chase the mechanical bunny alone.

For years, the cruelty to animals laws were not enforced to prevent the use of jackrabbits for greyhound training because rabbits were assumed (incorrectly) to be rodents, which Florida law excluded from protection (see box, Rabbit Teeth, page 55 for difference between rabbits and rodents).

HOW GREYHOUNDS ARE TRAINED TODAY

Today, jackrabbits cannot be used legally for training greyhounds. Although there are oldtimers who insist that a dog could run better if trained with live rabbits, and there are always rumors that live rabbits are sometimes used, most people familiar with dog racing agree that the training today is humane and that artificial lures have been substituted for live rabbits.

◁ △ The greyhound above is chasing a white rag controlled by the trainer. At left, the greyhound is jumping to catch a "squeaker lure," another of the substitutes for live rabbits.

Feral Cats and Dogs

DOMESTIC CAT
(Felis catus)

Many cats survive on their own in the wild in Florida, receiving no food from humans. These feral cats (meaning domestic cats surviving in the wild) generally live singly and have small, overlapping territories. They only come together for breeding.

Feral and domestic cats kill large numbers of wild animals. Feeding them does not seem to reduce their killing of normal prey. Mice are their primary food. Cats also eat small rabbits and fish. Most cats do not eat a lot of birds, but some cats develop a real taste for birds and come to prefer birds to rodents (cooked feathers are used as a taste enhancer in some commercial cat foods). In the wild, cats also eat a small amount of grass. Cats are picky eaters and will actually starve with food in front of them if they do not like it. Moreover, cats do not fight over food like dogs do.

Among mammals, cats are considered the best designed hunters in the world, because of their stealth, ease of movement, and excellent senses. Their bodies are well designed for running down prey and killing it efficiently.

Cats have padded feet to walk quietly, long whiskers so they can feel in the dark, twisting ears to pinpoint sounds, binocular vision, and great speed. Unlike the larger cats, the jaws of the domestic cat may lack the strength to crush vertebrae, but with their sharp canine teeth they can cut the spinal cord of prey without having to break the vertebrae.

Cats are color-blind like dogs, but unlike dogs, cats have terrific binocular vision. Their hearing is also very good. Cats can rotate their ears about 180 degrees, and they use sound to locate prey through triangulation, somewhat like binocular vision, especially at night. A cat's sense of smell is not nearly as developed as that of a dog. Cats use sound,

△ Domestic cat stalking wildlife prey. Cats may be responsible, at least in part, for the declining numbers of certain mammal, reptile, and bird species.

sight, and tactile senses to hunt, but they do not rely on scent as much as dogs.

A male in the wild marks territory by cheek rubbing, spraying urine, or defecating around the edges of its territory. Spraying urine is done primarily by male cats to communicate their territories to other animals.

When cats rub themselves against human legs, they leave secretions from glands around their face and mouth, used for marking. Scratching and extending of the claws is also usually marking behavior rather than claw sharpening. It leaves an oily substance from glands on the feet.

Outdoor cats, both feral and tame, are major predators of small mammals, birds, and reptiles throughout America, killing so many that they may endanger the survival of certain species. However, the wait-and-pounce hunting methods employed by cats are likely to be far more successful with small rodents and reptiles than with birds. Cats have been blamed for the decline or extinction of 20 native mammals in Australia. In Florida, cats are thought to have contributed to the decline of beach mice in several areas. We are still largely ignorant about the effects of cats on native wildlife, however, and more studies are needed to resolve the disputes that persist.

◁ ▷ Feral cats manage to feed themselves and survive with or without the help of man.

DOMESTIC DOG
(Canis familiaris)

All dogs have their origins in wolves, from the smallest chihuahua to the huge Saint Bernard. For this reason, the behavior of dogs is largely derived from the behavior of their wolf ancestors.

The dog is a social animal; it requires the company of other animals. It barks to call more dogs and likes to hunt in packs. The bark is also a canine alarm, meant to alert other members of the pack to danger. A barking dog is calling for reinforcements ("calling out the troops"), while a dog which is ready to attack usually doesn't give any warning. Hence the saying, "Barking dogs don't bite."

Dogs, like wolves, have a pecking order. There's always a boss or top dog, the alpha dog. Every dog knows exactly where it stands in its pack. When the alpha figure approaches, a lower dog puts its head down and may roll over, exposing its belly and throat, vulnerable areas of the body, in an act of submission.

Feral dogs may be serious pests, especially in rural areas. Unlike stray cats, wild dogs run in packs and are threats to livestock. They are especially fond of lambs and calves. Sometimes, however, what appears to be a pack of wild dogs may actually be unrestrained domestic males following a female in heat.

Feral dogs do have some effect on wildlife. They have been known to run down deer, but this is not so common in Florida. Wild dogs are more of a threat to deer in northern states where deer sometimes get bogged down in deep snow. However, Florida's Key deer are very vulnerable to attacks by packs of wild dogs.

THE HISTORY OF DOGS

In addition to being considered "man's best friend," dogs are used as work animals, or beasts of burden, for hunting, herding sheep, and carrying messages. But mostly dogs are kept for companionship, because they offer unconditional love.

The dog was the first mammal to be domesticated, perhaps as long as 10,000 years ago. It is believed that Stone Age men kept dogs as pets as well as to eat, so their domestication took place long before recorded history.

EATING DOGS

In many parts of the world, especially Asia, dogs are commonly eaten. The Chinese and the Filipinos are best known for this practice. In both cultures, dog meat is considered beneficial to the health, almost medicinal.

The ancient practice of eating dog meat has been embarrassing to a few modern governments. Several years ago, the National Enquirer ran a series of articles about the brutal manner in which dogs were brought to market and slaughtered in the Philippines. As a result, petitions with thousands of American signatures were presented to then President Marcos urging a halt to the practice. Before the Seoul Olympics, the Korean government attempted to eliminate the food stalls serving dog meat in the Korean capital. In 1992, an Australian government official created an international incident by jokingly associating a friend's lost pet with the recent visit of China's premier. The joke was reported in a newspaper and the Chinese protested, regarding the incident as a racial and cultural slur. The official nearly lost his job.

MAN
(Homo sapiens)

How does human behavior differ from that of the other mammals? The man in the photo obviously cares for his child, but a dog or a squirrel does the same without anyone having to teach it. A mammal's urge to care for its children is instinctive. So, how much of our behavior is the result of these instincts, and how much is the result of culture, learning and experience? Scientists have argued this point for centuries.

It is known that certain behaviors are more influenced by instinct than others. It is also known that the higher a mammal is on the evolutionary scale, the more its behavior is the result of learning rather than instinct. But there is always some influence from instinct, even for the most complex and advanced human behavior.

Formerly, it was thought that the ability to use tools and language clearly separated humans from the other mammals. Other traits thought to be strictly human were consciousness, learning ability, and emotion. Scientific study has shown that the gap between humans and their closest relatives, the primates, is not nearly as large as was once thought, but there is still much disagreement among scientists about the extent of the differences.

Research over the past 30 years with chimpanzees and other great apes has shown in remarkable ways that they have the ability to communicate using sign language or symbols, and that they make and use tools in the wild. Furthermore, like us, they do experience emotions of pleasure, fear, rage, sadness, depression, and anxiety to name a few.

Self-awareness, the ability to reflect on one's own condition, is generally perceived to be in the domain of human consciousness. This is a difficult trait to measure, but it is known that captive chimpanzees can recognize and examine themselves in mirrors. When asked to separate photos of animals, a captive chimp put pictures of dogs into one group and put pictures of herself in with a group of human photos. Jane Goodall, studying chimpanzees in the wild, reported that chimps are capable of intentionally deceiving other individuals, which suggests that they may be capable of self-awareness.

Primates are social animals, and familiarity with others is calming and creates an atmosphere in which play and learning can occur. Play and learning are important parts of both human and mammal societies.

Nevertheless, in spite of the similarities of human and primate behavior, great differences exist. Consider the highly developed human language and human achievements in science and art. Humans are capable of understanding the concept of events which will occur in the future and also those which have occurred in the distant past. We can understand the relationship of events. We are capable of transforming our environment to meet our needs for food and energy.

Both human and non-human mothers can recognize their infants by sight, but if the non-human mother gives inadequate care, or if she dies, the chance of survival for the infant is rather small. In human cultures, others can intervene to care for the young.

Aggression is often associated with animals, but no one can deny that it exists in all human cultures. In the animal world, aggression is linked with dominance and territoriality (and the resources a territory contains). Aggression is also linked with reproductive success. The dominant males with the best territories are the ones that get the females and are able to breed.

Aggression performs a number of functions in all animal communities which help a species adapt to its environment. In biological terms, aggression serves to allocate territories, form breeding hierarchies, and distribute resources. Within human societies, aggression is controlled somewhat by rituals such as laws, customs, treaties and truces, and organized competition. It is important to remember that genetically influenced behavior such as aggression is not always something precise. Genes contain blueprints for a range of behaviors that may be expressed in a wide variety of ways, depending upon environmental influences.

MAN IN FLORIDA

The earliest signs of humans in Florida date from 10,000 to 12,000 years ago, although they might have been here earlier. They probably followed the herds of big game that migrated southward across the North American continent. What is known of the early inhabitants of Florida has been pieced together by archeologists from remnants left behind: burial mounds, middens (garbage heaps) which contain remains of plants and animals eaten, bone and stone tools, and pieces of pottery.

The earliest inhabitants of Florida were the Paleo-Indians (the name given the earliest people known to inhabit North America). Little is known about them except that they were skilled nomadic hunters. Stone and ivory tools and weapons have been found at river sites, called "kill-sites," along with the remains of the large animals which were slain and butchered such as mammoths, mastodons, horses, bison, and giant land tortoises (see section on Florida's fossil mammals). The current known sites of these earliest known inhabitants are near deep water areas that would have been watering holes during a period when sea levels were lower and the environment was dryer. Animals would have gone there to drink, so these areas might have been ambush sites. These Indians also foraged for plants and smaller animals.

By about 6,500 B.C., hunting patterns changed with the disappearance of many of the larger mammals, and the Paleo-Indians became more settled. This next period, sometimes called the Archaic Period, is characterized by the use of a broader range of plants and animals. Mammal remains found in association with human settlement during this time period include deer, opossum, pocket gopher, rabbit, bear, and panther. Freshwater snails were taken from inland rivers and oysters and shellfish harvested in large numbers along both coasts. By about 2,000 B.C., the Indians had developed the technique of pottery making. The period from about 1,200 B.C. to the arrival of the Spanish was a time of more settled communities, with increasing reliance on agriculture in north Florida, where crops such as corn, beans, and squash were grown.

One of the most dramatic periods in the human history of Florida began with the arrival of the Spanish explorers and colonizers during the 15th century and continued into the British colonial times. During the first half of the 16th century, it is estimated that 100,000 people or more inhabited the state, divided into many different tribes. Most of the Indians of the northern part of the state were agriculturists, while in the south people still depended on hunting and gathering. This was a period of tremendous loss, not only in numbers of indigenous people, but in much of the old way of life. By 1710, the native population of Florida had been almost completely destroyed by diseases brought by the foreigners, against which the natives had no immunity, and also as the result of slavery and warfare. Because of the early and almost total destruction of many aboriginal groups, we may never know much about them. The loss of Florida Indians left areas of North-Central Florida vacant. In the early 1700s, the Creek Indians from Georgia, fleeing from the British in their own homeland, came to Florida. They became known as the Seminole Tribe, whose descendants are one of only two native American groups remaining in Florida

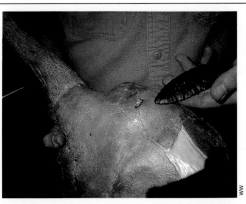

△ A bison skull with an embedded spear point was found in a north Florida river, providing solid evidence linking the Paleo-Indians with the now-extinct large mammals. The hand is holding a complete spear point of a similar type.

today. The second is the Miccosukee Tribe. They speak the same language as the Seminoles, but they claim to have an independent tribal history.

With increasing numbers of people and higher technology, man is changing the environment at an increasing rate and threatening the survival of many creatures. Florida is now the fourth most populous state in the country. Every year over 160,000 acres of Florida wild lands are destroyed. Many of Florida's endangered species are coastal or island creatures and the coasts and islands are the most desirable areas for development. With 44 million visitors and thousands of new residents each year, further loss of habitat is bound to occur. But even though humans have the capability for destruction, they also have the ability to make choices to protect what remains of our native environment.

MAN AND BEAST: MAN'S RELATIONSHIP WITH THE ANIMALS

Humans have been interacting with animals throughout their history on earth. The first images man created as art were animals drawn on cave walls. Even today hunting societies have elaborate rituals to appease the spirits of animals they have killed or to insure that wild animals on which they depend will always be plentiful. In our own society, the issue of hunting animals always provokes strong reactions from people on both sides.

Some animals arouse strong negative sentiments. Bats are often hated animals, associated with the occult and misfortune. However, they were considered Lords of the Night by the Aztecs and are considered good fortune by the Chinese. Cougars were considered "varments" by early settlers, but represented powerful symbols of a positive nature in the cultures of many Native American tribes.

What the role of animals in a society should be has been an open debate going back as far as the ancient Greeks. Some people felt that animals had souls while those at the other extreme believed that animals felt no pain and were no better than machines. In western society, humans considered themselves to be higher creatures and thus justified in using animals for any purpose, regardless of the suffering of the animal. In some societies certain animals were elevated to the status of dieties, while in others they were abused. Today, most people accept that animals can experience suffering, at least those with a highly developed nervous system, and many people believe that animals are worthy of our moral concern. But in our highly industrialized world, we have lost touch with nature and animals. Perhaps this one reason for the great popularity of zoos and the large increase in the number of pets.

The usefulness of protecting animals is being rediscovered through the conservation movement. With the destruction of much of the rain forests, it is estimated that by the end of the century, we will have lost one million species. While most agree that saving species is not of the same priority as feeding hungry people, it is important to consider the contributions of wild animals. Domestic animals have served man as storehouses of food and as work power. The mobility provided by the camel and the horse made possible exploration of new regions. Domestication of animals helped make our current large population possible. And today, many animals are very important to medical research.

Apart from direct scientific or economic benefits, the value of preserving the natural world for its beauty and wonder has never been more clear. But animals as revered as the elephant, as rare as the tiger, as endangered as the rhinoceros, and as beloved as the dolphin, to name only a few, are still being slaughtered for their relatively minor economic value.

TABLE OF CONTENTS:

CHIEF SEATTLE

A famous Native American, Chief Seattle of the Duwamps tribe in the Pacific Northwest, is reported to have described his feelings about nature and the environment in 1854 as follows:

"What is man without the beasts? If all the beasts were gone, man would die from loneliness of the spirit. For whatever happens to the beasts, soon happens to man."

In recent years, historians have debated whether Chief Seattle actually used these words, or whether the remarks were created by a newspaper reporter and attributed to him. In any case, no one can dispute the eloquence of these lines nor the fact that they are even more relevant today than the day they were spoken.

It is interesting to note that the city of Seattle was originally named Duwamps after the Duwamps Tribe which lived in that area. Later, after Chief Seattle befriended the settlers, the city was renamed in his honor.